Deeply thoughtful about ⬛⬛⬛⬛⬛ so
drawing on the best of th ⬛⬛⬛⬛⬛ *trable* is
for every man and every ⬛⬛⬛⬛⬛ f work.

STEVEN GARBER
Principal of the Washington Institute for Faith, Vocation & Culture and
author of *Visions of Vocation*

A greatly needed resource that pastorally weaves together biblical
teaching and rich theology in the context of a wide diversity of
occupations.

DAVID H. KIM
Executive director, Center for Faith & Work

John Van Sloten gives us eyes to see that our work is not only
designed to serve others but is also essentially formative on our
journey to greater Christlikeness. I highly recommend this book.

TOM NELSON
Author of *Work Matters*

All work is meant to be God honoring. I have long believed that
and taught it. But in this marvelous book John Van Sloten brings it
all alive for me in new ways. I will be ready to read a parable from
the Lord every time I see a sanitation worker or a Walmart greeter!

RICHARD MOUW
President Emeritus, Fuller Theological Seminary

John Van Sloten's book presents a wide-ranging and deeply
practical theology of vocation, helping readers see how God speaks
and works through jobs we might never have thought were "sacred."
A treasure trove of insights and a great resource for the church.

BRETT McCRACKEN
Author of *Hipster Christianity*, *Gray Matters*, and *Uncomfortable*

Filled with startling insights and fascinating characters, Van Sloten's
book will help you see that what you do Monday through Friday
truly is a sacred calling, one in which God wants to speak to you
and to the rest of the world. Highly recommended!

DREW DYCK
Senior editor of CTPastors.com and author of *Yawning at Tigers*

Here are stories of regular people who are discovering the bubbling
ferment of God's Kingdom in their callings and vocations. Read this
and be encouraged that the Spirit really is out ahead of us in our
work lives and callings.

ALAN ROXBURGH
President of The Missional Network

JOHN VAN SLOTEN
EVERY JOB
WHAT WALMART GREETERS, NURSES,

A PARABLE

AND ASTRONAUTS TELL US ABOUT GOD

NavPress

A NavPress resource published in alliance
with Tyndale House Publishers, Inc.

NAVPRESS○®

NavPress is the publishing ministry of The Navigators, an international Christian organization and leader in personal spiritual development. NavPress is committed to helping people grow spiritually and enjoy lives of meaning and hope through personal and group resources that are biblically rooted, culturally relevant, and highly practical.

For more information, visit www.NavPress.com.

Every Job a Parable: What Walmart Greeters, Nurses, and Astronauts Tell Us about God

Copyright © 2017 by John Van Sloten. All rights reserved.

A NavPress resource published in alliance with Tyndale House Publishers, Inc.

NAVPRESS and the NAVPRESS logo are registered trademarks of NavPress, The Navigators, Colorado Springs, CO. *TYNDALE is* a registered trademark of Tyndale House Publishers, Inc. Absence of ® in connection with marks of NavPress or other parties does not indicate an absence of registration of those marks.

The Team:
Don Pape, Publisher
David Zimmerman, Acquisitions Editor
Dean Renninger, Designer

Cover photograph of astronaut copyright © Tim Bird/Getty Images. All rights reserved.

Author photo by Martin Glyn Jones, copyright © 2017. All rights reserved.

Anecdotal illustrations in this book are true to life and are included with the permission of the persons involved. All other illustrations are composites of real situations, and any resemblance to people living or dead is purely coincidental.

For information about special discounts for bulk purchases, please contact Tyndale House Publishers at csresponse@tyndale.com, or call 1-800-323-9400.

Cataloging-in-Publication Data is available.

ISBN 978-1-63146-548-2

Printed in the United States of America

22	21	20	19	18	17
6	5	4	3	2	1

*For my dad, who for decades faithfully
caught the 7:37 morning train to work.*

Contents

Finding God at Work

They will not work in vain.

ISAIAH 65:23, NLT

....

God is more present at your work than you know. And I think he wants you to know that. God wants you to see that he is there and that his Spirit is moving *in* you, *through* you, and *all around* you as you do your job. God wants you to know him in all you do—including the third of your life that you spend working.

Over the past five years, I have preached Sunday sermons on many different vocations: on astronauts, auto mechanics, emergency room doctors, hairstylists, investment bankers, Walmart greeters, engineers, firefighters, accountants, electricians, forensic psychologists, city mayors, painters, musicians, parents, carpenters, composers, glass blowers, Olympic swimmers, hockey players, major-league pitchers, emergency response helicopter pilots, geophysicists, nephrologists, geologists, audiologists, optometrists, florists, epigenetics researchers, neuroscientists, residential landlords, real estate developers, software developers, oil industry executives, molecular biologists, radiation physicists, police officers, photographers, journalists, bakers, nurses, restaurant servers, teachers, human resources managers, development workers, sanitation workers, custom automobile restorers, and farmers.

As I have engaged all of these jobs, I have realized that each is a kind of *parable*—a lived-out story within which and through which God speaks in multiple ways. Parables were a key aspect of Jesus' teachings—he depicted God's Kingdom through stories about laborers, farmers, jewel merchants, kings, judges, managers, builders, general-store keepers, landlords, and vineyard owners. He used these stories, the Bible tells us, as a kind of advanced class for his most responsive audiences: "To those who listen to my teaching, more understanding will be given, and they will have an abundance of knowledge. But for those who are not listening, even what little understanding they have will be taken away from them" (Matthew 13:12, NLT).

For years my view of how Jesus' parables worked was limited. I understood them to be narrative tools for the conveyance of moral and ethical truth, stories with a built-in spiritual lesson. I still believe this. But lately I've come to realize that the *created elements* of his stories—the down-to-earthness, the real-life content, ordinary people doing ordinary things—also carried revelatory weight. Jesus was telling stories filled with things he made (soil, seeds, agriculture, and farmers), things that revealed something about their maker. Parables, in many ways, pointed to God's revelation via creation. When Jesus wrapped a parable around a particular vocation, he was affirming the creational goodness of that job.

I think Jesus is still doing the same today—through the parable that is your job.

That's what this book is about: understanding how Jesus is speaking directly *to* you (via your personal experience of work) and how he is speaking *through* you (to the broader world). It's about hearing God's creational words through created things: the rocks a geologist explores, the cars a mechanic fixes, the lights an electrician installs, the customers a retail worker serves. The "stuff" we work with interacts and commingles with the "stuff" of our work itself, leading to an enriched vocational experience of God.

As you read this book you'll encounter God's revelation through various vocational parables, as shared with me by the people I interviewed. You'll learn how a firefighter's passion is like God's, how the nature of automotive restoration uniquely reflects the renewing mind of God, how the cultural product of the culinary arts reveals something of the hospitable heart of God, and how a geophysicist's search for subterranean truth informs humanity's collective search for God's truth.

And you'll start to see how these present-day job-based parables are a lot like the New Testament parables Jesus told.

Throughout the Bible, in fact, God accomplished his will and made himself known through real people doing real work: creating, building, tending, leading, managing, restoring, and filling the world with good things.

This is how God worked in the past. This is how God works today!

Jesus is speaking the parable that is your vocational life right now—a *word* from God that is meant to be *read* by others and *experienced* by you. Imagine your job charged with this kind of mystical, God-revealing potential.

Sacred.

Holy.

A RENEWED VOCATIONAL IMAGINATION

The purpose of this book is to help kindle a new kind of vocational imagination, to help you experience God at work more, and to help you read the parable that is your job.

It is for people who trust that God is at work everywhere.

It is for those who believe that God is the Maker of heaven and earth; that he holds human history in his hands; and that the sociological, cultural, scientific, and technological developments of our age have been brought to this time and place with intent.

This book is for those who believe that the kind of work they do, the talents they have been given, and the things they will accomplish are held in God's hands, and that he has a purpose for it all—even if that purpose is unclear, appears to be falling short, or is seemingly out of reach.

I believe God intended work to be a means through which we can know him, experience him, and relate to him—all in the context of his providential unfolding of history.

After all, we are made in the image of a God who works.

He is the one who first imagined the cosmos: quarks, muons, and atoms; basic elements, chemical bonds, and genetics; germination, photosynthesis, and capillary action. The God who creatively designed the universe and in whose mind the complexities of all physical reality first took shape.

The God who holds and mysteriously guides all of the ways of culture: business, government, education, science, agriculture, the arts, service industries, sport, and leisure—all in accordance with his good and perfect will. The God who providentially cares for human culture, seeding in us the capacity to flourish and presiding over our innovations, our language, art, and math and all their extrapolations, to "fill the earth and govern it" (Genesis 1:28, NLT). The God who inspired early iterations of arithmetic, knowing that they would one day become calculus—and then a suspension bridge! The God who led the ancient Greeks to ponder human nature so that the science of psychology would one day have a footing and that organizational behavior principles could later develop and enable business to thrive.

God made everything out of nothing. Now he is taking what he has made and making more out of it. One crucial means by which he is accomplishing this is through *work*.

His work and ours.

As you read these words, you might be thinking that all of this is a bit of a stretch. Is God really *that* involved with everything that fills creation? Are all things really playing out on purpose and for a greater good? What about corrupt governments, businesses, and cultural practices, and all of the other twisting, polluting, exploiting, and perverting impacts of sin? What about those who endure terrible working conditions? What connection could all of these broken things possibly have with God's revelation? Isn't there a line between what God does and what human beings do? How do you separate the two? How in the world can you claim to discern God's revelation through all of this confusion?[1]

By doing the same thing you do when you read the Bible.

In the Bible, God is *very much* present in even the most broken circumstances. Through messed-up people living in a damaged world, God's redemptive plan is still very much playing out. The Scriptures tell a story about a God who gets his work done despite these complexities—through murderers, betrayers, chronic liars, adulterous kings, prostitutes, leaders of unbelieving nations, and countless hubris-filled hearts. Through broken people and cultures, God's will is done and he speaks his word: freeing slaves; saving people; building up nations; judging others; developing good communities, cities, and cultures; and even celebrating the fruit of those cultures.

If we can read our jobs as we read our Bibles, then we'll be able to discern what God is revealing there. If we can move past what many of us believe in theory—that God is present everywhere, mysteriously getting his will done via human agency (despite the reality of evil) in a redemptive and self-revealing way—and if we can listen for God's very specific word at work, then I believe that with the Spirit's help, we'll hear it.

If God speaks through all of the brokenness in the Bible, then surely he does the same today, speaking through our work and culture. Imagine letting God be God at this level of detail in your life![2]

THE PARABLE OF AN ASTRONAUT

One of the most beautiful stories to rise out of the ashes of 9/11 came to us through the at-work words of American astronaut Frank Culbertson. As smoke was pouring from the Twin Towers on that fateful day, Commander Culbertson was looking down on Manhattan from the International Space Station, filming what he saw. While he knew something horrible was happening on the ground, he also saw something more. Through a crackling NASA communication link he spoke these hopeful words:

> I just wanted the folks to know that their city still looks very beautiful from space. I know it's very difficult for everybody in America right now. The country still looks good, and for New Yorkers, your city still looks great from up here.[3]

Those words were comforting. And they were true! If you look at the NASA video, you can see that most of Manhattan was still standing; the ocean, rivers, and tributaries were still beautifully held within their boundaries; the sky was brilliantly clear; and millions of people on that island were still alive and safe—along with hundreds of millions more in the rest of the country.

That perspective could come only from someone who saw things from above.

As I watched that video and listened to that astronaut's words, I couldn't help but wonder whether this is how an omniscient, omnipresent, all-powerful, and eternal God sees our world. Could it be that if we just stood back far enough and had more of his perspective, we, too, would be able to see that there is still good going on in our lives, families, and jobs—even when it doesn't seem that way?

From heaven the LORD looks down
    and sees all mankind:
from his dwelling place he watches
    all who live on earth—
he who forms the hearts of all,
    who considers everything they do.

PSALM 33:13-15

Surely God suffered with us on 9/11. But perhaps he also had this other view of reality to share: through an astronaut bearing his image, seeing the whole picture from above and speaking encouraging words from above, his job a kind of parable spoken by God for just such a time as that.

When the 1968 Apollo 8 mission to the moon first turned its camera back on Earth and humanity saw an earthrise for the first time, everything changed. The moment was so compelling that the astronauts could do nothing less than read the creation account from the book of Genesis via live broadcast. This was the first time a human being saw Earth as a planet, as a whole. This view brought us new perspective, awareness, and humility. One astronaut said, "That may well have been the most important reason we went."[4]

It's called the "Overview Effect": a kind of God's-eye view of reality. While God certainly sees our physical planet from a perspective that is beyond ours, I'm thinking that the same is true when it comes to seeing reality in relation to our environment, economic and social structures, and vocations. There is more going on than meets our eyes.

This kind of *seeing* is foundational for this book: a larger perspective that sees what work was originally meant to be and what it will one day fully be, even as things may be tough on the ground right now. A deeper look into the creational good that makes up what you do, a longer view on the significance of your job, all leading to a richer experience of God at work.

After all, "The earth is the LORD's, and everything in it, the world, and all who live in it" (Psalm 24:1). Our world belongs to God, and even though it is fallen, none of it has fallen beyond God's reach. Because God is good, Saint Augustine tells us, there "cannot be a nature in which there is no good."[5]

It's this vocational good that this book is seeking out. The process may feel a bit idealistic at times, but it has to. To name where God is at work in our vocations *is* to name what's still good, true, noble, and right in this world. So allow yourself some intentional naïveté as you engage the ideas in this book. When you start to name God's good at work, it will grow, displacing all that is currently falling short.

God wants this for you. As any good boss or mentor would, he wants to come alongside you and show you the way. You are an apprentice of the greatest artist, engineer, planner, mathematician, assembler, analyst, scientist, laborer, administrator, and server imaginable. Just as a novice watches every move of a journeyman, you are called to fix your senses on your Master—learning at every turn, observing his ways, smiling at the way he thinks, being astonished at what he knows, feeling gratitude for the patient way he teaches, getting excited about the beautiful thing, the necessary thing, or the ordinary thing you are making together.[6]

THE COMMON GOOD?

Recently there has been a lot of talk about the idea of working for the *common good*—for the good of your neighbor, society, classmate, environment, and world. A lot of people think this is the ultimate objective when it comes to work.

While working for the common good is an important part of a balanced vocational worldview, it is not *all* that work is meant for. In fact, sometimes it can get in the way and become an impediment to work's chief purpose: a real-time knowing and experiencing of God. When this happens, our jobs can become nothing more than a "works-based" means of vocational salvation. Work becomes something that is based on *what we do for God*, as opposed to *who we are before him*.

This is not to say that our work and faith shouldn't materially impact our world or that we can't know and experience God in the *doing*—they should, and we can. But all of our good works must be born out of a more primary and gracious starting point, out of a place where we intimately relate to and experience the person of God: *on* the job. Our good work is meant to be a grateful response to a grace-filled encounter with God.

Jesus taught that there are basically two laws we need to keep in order to flourish as human beings: "'Love the Lord your God with all your heart and with all your soul and with all your mind.' This is the first and greatest commandment. And the second is like it: 'Love your neighbor as yourself'" (Matthew 22:37-39).

Love God first and foremost, with all you've got; then, *out of that love*, work for the common good.

These two laws are not mutually exclusive. They are symbiotic—mutually fulfilling and interdependent. Love of God shapes and informs love of neighbor. You can't fully love your neighbor (or yourself) unless you are in a loving relationship with God. You won't know *why* and *when* and *how* to work for the common good unless you are doing it out of a "right then and there" *working* love of God, out of his "just in time" ethical, wise, creative, and mindful presence.

The reverse is true as well: Only by loving your neighbor (working for the common good) will you be able to fully love God. Work concretizes your faith; it puts God's words into action. We need to be doing both at the same time—loving God and loving our neighbor—to be fully alive.

And it all starts with a loving, knowing experience of God.[7]

MAKING ROOM

In order to make room for that experience, we need to keep God's priorities in order.

Knowing God at work is more than just believing that God gave you your job, more than just understanding that he is the source of vocational morals or ethics, and more than just viewing him as the one you witness about or ultimately work for or give a portion of your earnings back to. He is more than just a God whom you serve. To know God at work is even more than just working for the common good.

While all of these ways of connecting faith and vocation are valid, none get to the *core* of where God meets work— those real-time experiences of God when "out of the blue" inspiration hits you, when a huge challenge confronts you and you find another physical or cognitive gear, or when you are so caught up in the flow of what you are doing that you lose all sense of time and space.

If you are already experiencing God on the job this way, put this book down and get back to work! But if not, or if you want to have a deeper experience of God at work, then read on.

My hope is that, through the stories of many workers from various vocations, this book will provide you with a set of spiritual practices (a *lectio vocatio*) that will teach you how to read your job and will enable you to discern where God is speaking to you, through you, and through others at work.

PART ONE

WHAT DOES IT MEAN TO IMAGE GOD?

ALL WORK MATTERS

WHAT A FLYER DELIVERY PERSON, A WALMART GREETER,
A FORENSIC PSYCHOLOGIST, AND A RESIDENTIAL LANDLORD
TEACH US ABOUT THE VALUE OF ALL WORK

Surely the LORD is in this place, and I was not aware of it.

JACOB, IN GENESIS 28:16

....

In the book of Genesis, there is a story about the Old
Testament patriarch Jacob, who, while on a journey, stopped
in a seemingly ordinary, middle-of-nowhere place to rest for
the night. He slept on the ground, using a rock as a pillow.
And there he had a dream in which he met God.

In that dream, God made hope-filled
promises to Jacob: that he would be
Jacob's God, give him a place to make
a life, and bless him in such a way that
everyone around him would be blessed
through his presence. When Jacob awoke

FEATURED IN THIS CHAPTER:
• Flyer delivery person
• Walmart greeter
• Forensic psychologist
• Residential landlord

from his sleep, he thought, "Surely the LORD is in this place,
and I was not aware of it. . . . How awesome is this place!
This is none other than the house of God; this is the gate of
heaven" (Genesis 28:16-17).

Far too often people journey through their vocational

lives with no expectation of ever meeting God there. For one reason or another, they have lost sight of God's everywhere presence. Some think their jobs are too insignificant, ordinary, and middle-of-nowhere. Others think that what they do couldn't possibly connect to the ways of God and that there is nothing of God's goodness in their jobs. Some have never even considered or imagined connecting with God at work. Work is work; God is at church.

A few years ago, I had a conversation with a woman who delivered flyers in our neighborhood. She was no more than five feet tall and in her seventies. Two or three times a week, she would pull a heavy, homemade wooden wagon filled with flyers through our streets—up and down the many hills; over curbs; through rain, snow, and heat. Every time I saw her working, I was amazed and also a bit saddened by how difficult that kind of job must have been for an older woman. Often I would say hi and talk to her as we passed on the street. One day I decided to stop and have a real conversation.

We talked about her work. She told me that she had been delivering flyers in my neighborhood for over twenty years; this was her last day on the job. Twenty years! Wow!

I told her that I had been watching her do her work since I had moved into the area. "I can't believe you have been strong enough to pull this heavy thing." I grabbed the handle of her wagon and pulled it a few inches; it must have weighed fifty pounds! She said that it wasn't so bad, once you got used to it.

I asked her why she had decided to stop work now. She said that over the past year, she had come to realize that she just couldn't do the job anymore—"You just *know* these things." She was thinking of working at Walmart instead. "At least I'll be warm in the winter."

This was the day of her retirement. Was anyone going to throw a party? Present her with a gold watch? Say a few kind words? I knew I had to say something and recognize her for what she had given. Someone had to thank her.

So I thanked her. "You know, you must have helped thousands of people in this community save money over the years with all those coupons and sales flyers. Thank you for that!"

She paused, took it in for a second, and then said, "Yeah, I guess so." Then she smiled. I asked her name; she told me it was Colleen. I introduced myself, shook her hand, and wished her all the best in her retirement.

I continued on my walk, and she picked up her wagon handle, looked over her address list one more time, and pulled her stack of flyers to the next house.

Too many times over the years, I have pulled a thick wad of advertisements out of my mailbox and felt a bit of frustration with the flyer industry. All that wasted paper and recycling hassle—all that consumer pressure. But for Colleen, this was her job—her life, in some large part. After our "retirement conversation," I hoped I could engage my job with as much dignity, perseverance, and strength.

I have to admit, I was kind of surprised that I was able and willing to articulate some of God's goodness to Colleen in relation to her work. As I look back, it had a lot to do with what I was feeling in that moment: a deep compassion, bordering on love, for her as a human being. As I looked at her from that perspective, I was able to see value in who she was and what she did. I was able to see where God was working through her.

Surely God was already in that place, and I was unaware of it.

Surely God feels a love that brings dignity to every human being doing every kind of job, no matter how big or small.

There is a Latin phrase used by the ancient mystics: *ubi amor, ibi oculus*—"Where there is love, there is seeing."[1] God is love, so he must see everything. As maker and keeper of all people and things, God knows the real value, the eternal significance, of even the most seemingly insignificant work. "With God nothing is empty of meaning," wrote the early church father Irenaeus.[2] As people of faith, we worship "a creator who loves us enough to seek us in the most mundane circumstances of our lives."[3] There is no job so boring that it would disinterest God, because there is no person whom God does not love and see.

God is whispering truth and meaning in the most ordinary and small places. In fact, those are often the places where God *especially* shows up. Given what the Bible reveals about how he came to us as a baby and was born into very humble circumstances, it seems clear that God often chooses to show up in middle-of-nowhere places. Remember the times where Jesus reached out to and included the last and least? He chose untrained fishermen to be his disciples—ordinary laborers to deliver the world's greatest message.

So if you work at a seemingly ordinary job, don't let that lead you to believe that it is ordinary to God. God is at work and can be known anywhere.

We humans have created a kind of vocational hierarchy:

White-collar is better than blue-collar; leading others trumps following them; high salaries outshine low salaries; managing beats out serving; highly educated is superior to less educated; high-profile is better than behind-the-scenes. While there is nothing wrong with high-level leadership, business success, or making a good salary (Jacob, for example, was materially blessed), these false assumptions undermine the vocational experience of many workers, lowering their job satisfaction and leaving them with little or no expectation of experiencing God at work. If you can't love an ordinary job, how can you ever find God there?

The first time I met Shirley, she was greeting at our neighborhood Walmart. When I asked her whether she would be willing to do a video interview for a sermon I was preaching, she initially didn't want to draw any attention to herself. For Shirley, greeting was all about others. "I like people," she said. "I want to help them find the department they are looking for, have a better day . . . by smiling or just saying hello . . . [or] by getting them a shopping cart." She loved her job, and she loved serving. Shirley did for others what she would want them to do for her. Many of the customers who walked by that morning knew her name.

Once she realized I was serious about wanting to understand more about her work, she consented to an interview. Following the interview, with the camera off, we had a more personal conversation. I discovered her deeper side. She had been through a lot, yet she seemed so content and at peace. She knew herself!

Driving home I thought, *What a wonderful human being!* And then I felt ashamed.

The day before the interview, I had come up with the idea of asking the Walmart manager if I could be a greeter for a morning. What better way to understand the job? I quickly nixed the idea because I worried that someone I knew might see me there. Yet here was Shirley—a seventy-seven-year-old woman who didn't go to church but still believed in God— imaging Christ in a way that I couldn't.

At one point in the Gospels, Jesus washed his disciples' feet (John 13:1-17). Shirley does the same every time she humbly puts a Walmart customer before herself.

According to the Bible, God is a God who serves. Selflessness in the smallest things is indicative of his nature. So whenever anybody humbly serves another in a selfless way at their job or anywhere else, they are, in a very real sense, imitating Christ. I believe that the Holy Spirit is moving through them, giving them the humility to kneel and to look up to others. And through that humble act, they become more human. This must be why Shirley knew herself so well; God's humility was moving through her.

Theologian Cornelius Plantinga wrote,

According to God's intelligence, the way to thrive is to help others to thrive; the way to flourish is to cause others to flourish; the way to fulfill yourself is to spend yourself. Jesus himself tried to get this lesson across to his disciples by washing their feet, hoping to ignite a little of the trinitarian life in them. The idea is that if—in a band of disciples, in a family, in a college—people encourage each other, pour out interest and goodwill upon each other, favor each other with blessings customized to fit the other person's need, what transpires is a lovely burst of shalom.[4]

For weeks after that Walmart interview, I kept seeing an image of Shirley's aged hands pushing those shopping carts— a great-grandmother doing all that physical work for other able-bodied people, standing all day, greeting customers where they were, selflessly incarnating the hospitable heart of God. She didn't judge those who walked through the door. And it made a difference.

Now, when I reconnect with Shirley at Walmart, I tell her about how her story continues to be told via online sermon video downloads, and she glows. My prayer is that through the attention I have shown her, she will catch a glimpse of a God who sees her as well. Perhaps she will even experience his smiling presence every time she smiles at another and a foretaste of his goodness in the goodness she already feels in greeting others.

There is no job too small for God's presence. But for some workers, it is not the size of their job that is the problem; it is the nature, scope, and content. What they do seems very far removed from what God would do. Aren't there just some jobs where God's goodness is unlikely to be found?

FORENSIC PSYCHOLOGY

A while ago, a forensic psychologist told me that while there are many jobs where God's truth and goodness are clearly evident, in work like his—diagnosing and then bearing bad news about what is often irreparable impairment—God's presence is a lot harder to find. How could this kind of vocation ever image God?

Later he sent me an e-mail further detailing the nature of his work: "My job essentially consists of identifying neuro-cognitive impairment (i.e., impaired concentration, memory, speech/language, decision-making) associated with brain pathology (disease or injury) and predictive of disability." In other words, 99 percent of the time, he's giving people bad news: "The only good news would be if an individual is less impaired than he/she thought."

As I considered his e-mail, the words of God through the prophet Jeremiah came to mind:

This is what the LORD says:

"Your wound is incurable,
    your injury beyond healing.
There is no one to plead your cause,
    no remedy for your sore,
    no healing for you."
JEREMIAH 30:12-13

We live in a sin-corrupted and broken world. People's bodies and minds and families and communities are not what they are supposed to be, not what God intended when he first made them. Life falls short—all of it, including our work.

But this psychologist's work was not devoid of the presence of God. Nothing can be completely so. While his particular profession may deal with more brokenness than most, God is still very much at work there.

A forensic psychologist is made in the image of a God who sometimes brings terrible news: "Your wound is incurable, your injury beyond healing. This won't ever go away or get better." Sometimes the truth is difficult to hear. Nobody wants to be the bearer of bad news. And yet, there is still something very right—something Godlike!—about the act of naming fallen reality for what it is.

The forensic psychologist started to do the math himself. "Does a person whose job it is to search for pathology work in a role similar to the Holy Spirit, who convicts of brokenness, sin, and impurity?" he wrote me. "In turn, the pathologist is intimately reminded and convicted by the Holy Spirit of what is unholy and the need for healing, remediation, reconciliation, and resurrection. Unlike jobs filled with the beauty of creation, the pathologist is reminded daily of the futility of our attempts to be whole without God, never able to forget that we, and the otherwise beautiful creation around us, [are] fallen, and [remain] so without the *hope* of resurrection."

As I read his note, what came to mind were the words of Jesus, as recorded by his disciple John:

> When [the Holy Spirit] comes, he'll expose the error
> of the godless world's view of sin, righteousness,
> and judgment: He'll show them that their refusal
> to believe in me [Jesus] is their basic sin; that
> righteousness comes from above, where I am with
> the Father, out of their sight and control; that

> judgment takes place as the ruler of this godless
> world is brought to trial and convicted.
>
> JOHN 16:8-11, MSG

Wow! A pretty harsh diagnosis from Jesus! Our godless world isn't seeing things straight. Our basic sin is that we don't believe that Jesus is who he says he is and that what he says comes from God the Father. The Spirit's role is to bring judgment, trial, and conviction.

According to the Bible, Jesus is the one *through* whom and *for* whom all things were made—the one who is now holding all things together, including you and what you do. We say we believe these basic truths about who Jesus is, and yet most of the time we go about our daily work as though he is not there. We barely give him the time of day. We pay him lip service by limiting his presence at work to issues of morality, work ethic, or witnessing. In many ways, perhaps out of ignorance or willful denial or sloth, we refuse to give him lordship over our jobs. We forget that Jesus calls his followers to give their *whole* lives to him, every moment of every day. Christ loves us so much he could never be satisfied with anything less.

In order for us to really understand our vocational condition, Jesus sends his Holy Spirit to convict us, to name our working shortfalls for what they are, so that we will know how incurable our wounds are. Maybe then we might be humbled and inspired enough to look beyond ourselves for some kind of saving.

How we work (and live) is falling short of the glory of God. The Holy Spirit's job is to illumine this fact, even as a forensic psychologist's job is to incisively identify and name brokenness in our brains.

So how exactly does our experience of work fall short? If work, at its best, is meant to be a place where we experience God more fully and know Jesus for who he really is, then where exactly are things breaking down?

When it comes to getting the diagnosis right, the forensic psychologist has a laserlike focus. "I do not represent [the client]," he said. "What I do is represent brains, cognitive problems, depression, anxiety, [and] post-traumatic stress. I represent those things and will represent *them* very well." He wasn't a therapist, nor was he there to empathize or have a relationship with the client. The only reason he engaged his clients was to nail down the nature of the problem. "Getting it right is critical," he said.

Like this forensic psychologist, God isn't soft on sin. Yes, he loves us. But his holiness requires a perfect objectivity and a precise and unrelenting conviction when it comes to identifying sin's corrupting nature. God would agree with the psychologist's words: "Without conviction you can't bring about change."

And it is a conviction regarding a *condition* that is critical. Yes, sin manifests itself volitionally—we make poor choices— but sin is also very much a condition, something we don't really *do* and can't fix ourselves. Just as a brain-damaged person doesn't know any better, so too we don't know any better.

For the patient who hears the forensic psychologist's diagnosis for the first time, the news can be both unsettling and freeing—unsettling in terms of having to acknowledge the permanence of the condition, and freeing in that a person might for the first time understand his or her situation in a new way. They may think, *Okay, there is a reason that I feel this way, that I respond to life this way! Now it makes more sense. I have a brain injury that I can't fix. But this is not all that I am.*[5]

On this side of God's new creation, work is always going to be less than it could be. Like a brain-injured person, its condition falls short in a permanent way. For those of us who are still hoping to find that perfect career, this may be hard to hear—but it is also freeing to realize. *Okay. This is why I feel the way I do. Now I can start to learn to adapt.*

By conceding that work can never "save you" or "make you" or fulfill all of your desires and passions, you free yourself from idolatrous, unsustainable, and ultimately futile pursuits.

Acknowledging our vocational condition can also bring some peace when it comes to falling short of our goals and dreams. We are made to dream big dreams, but as Abraham Kuyper reminds us, there are limits to what human work can accomplish. We can shape and process things that already exist, but *only God* creates: "No human artist can create substance and splendor in reality; only God can do that."[6]

Knowing our vocational condition can be freeing. The intractability of the problem can, of course, also offer a strong impetus to search for some external force (not affected by the condition) to free us. Free us from a world that says delivering flyers couldn't possibly matter to anybody. Free us from stigmatizing and prejudging whether a Walmart greeter's job has meaning. Free us from the voices that tell us that God is only at work at certain jobs, in the good things, and that he couldn't possibly be found in places of pathology.

A LANDLORD

When I first met Sam Kolias, one of Canada's biggest residential landlords, I was excited to explore his vocation and see what it might reveal about God. Having previously read that Sam was a man of faith, I jumped right in and told him that I believe our world belongs to God and that, in a way, we all are God's tenants.

I was saying all of this to a man who was closer than most to understanding the scope of God's home-providing heart. Who else provides housing for over fifty thousand people?

For Sam, his company was providing more than just a physical house; it provided a home, a place where people could feel a sense of belonging and community. Being a landlord was so much more than bricks and mortar to him. Sam was coming out of his chair as he spoke about these core passions and his deepest joys.

In an interview with a national newspaper, Sam said, "I was raised in an environment where you help your neighbour and you treat them like you want to be treated. That's our number-one rule as a company. It's in our policy manual and we ask everybody on our team to always think of the other person like they want to be thought of themselves."[7] Sam embodies the Golden Rule; his entire organization does as well. In so doing, they image the love of God.

Sam told me about some of the philanthropic work being done by his company. As he spoke, he turned to look up a quotation from Mother Teresa. I can still picture Sam, with his back turned to me, looking up the quotation on one of three computers behind his desk. The other two had all kinds of financial data, graphs, and charts on their screens. As he pulled up the quotation and read it, I distinctly remember thinking, *How does that quote from Mother Teresa connect to all of the information on those other two computer screens? What does the innate nature of the business of being a landlord say about the nature of God?*

Sam and I discussed these questions. Doing work in a loving way is paramount. God is honored when we work the way he does. And he's also honored by the passions, skills, and aptitudes that bring love to fruition. Sam's deep joy in providing a home for others (clearly evidenced in the many stories he told) images God's joy. His entrepreneurial, make-something-out-of-nothing passion reveals the God who created everything out of nothing so that we all would have a place to live. Sam's leadership of a team that manages and creates large systems enabling residents to live safely and in peace mirrors the Spirit's leadership in providentially holding our planet. Sam's passion to lead and inspire others to live out his landlording vision reflects God's world-leading heart.

As we spoke, I was taken aback by all of the unique ways Sam images God through his work as a landlord—a heart filled with the love of God for others, fully in sync with the God-given mind and skills of an entrepreneur.

God works through every good facet of a landlord's job.

He works through every good facet of *any* job, big or small, extraordinary or ordinary, hands-on or cerebral, difficult or easy. Every job is filled with pointers to his presence.

LECTIO VOCATIO

It is interesting to note how "finding God at work" can be a challenge for those on either end of the employment ladder. It is easy to dismiss the routine jobs of some workers as too "bottom-rung" to really matter to God, and for those at the top, it is easy to believe that philanthropy is the only evidence of God's vocational presence.

Either extreme misses out—as does the belief that some jobs are just *holier* than others. The truth is that there is no job where God is not present in some way. Yet many of us are convinced of the opposite.

So what is your excuse?

My job doesn't directly help people. (But does it image God? Check out the next chapter.)

My job doesn't make a difference. (Be patient and make sure you read the final chapter.)

My job pollutes, or feeds consumerism, or in some other way causes anti-flourishing. (How can God use you to make this part of his world new?)

My job is devoid of anything good or godly. (Reread the part of this chapter about the forensic psychologist.)

My job is devoid of God's presence because of how messed up *I* am. (Make sure you read chapter 7.)

My job _____ .

IMAGING GOD WITH YOUR WHOLE BEING

WHAT TRADES AND TRANSLATORS TEACH US ABOUT EXPERIENCING GOD IN EVERY IMAGE-BEARING MOMENT

I was sometimes quieted at the sight of a gang of conduit entering a large panel in an industrial setting, bent into nestled, flowing curves, with varying offsets, that somehow terminated in the same plane. This was a skill so far beyond my abilities that I felt that I was in the presence of some genius, and the man who bent that conduit surely imagined this moment of recognition as he worked.

MATTHEW CRAWFORD, *SHOP CLASS AS SOULCRAFT*

We all are made in the image of a God who works: the one who created everything, rested from his work, tends and keeps all that he has made, and now continues to fill creation through us.

Each of us, through whatever work we do, is made to image God. When we get it right (and none of us ever fully do) and when our lives are in sync with the way God made us to work (and none of us ever fully are), every part of who we are—our imaginations, motivations, passions, hopes, dreams, skills, and abilities

FEATURED IN THIS CHAPTER:
- Electrician
- Craftsperson
- Automotive mechanic
- Tradesperson
- Language translator

(even though all of our parts fall short)—has the potential to image him.

Theologian Herman Bavinck spoke about our image bearing as being *that* all-encompassing:

> To be human is to be an image-bearer of God,
> created in his likeness and originally righteous
> and holy. The whole person is the image of the
> whole deity. There has been extensive debate in
> the Christian church about the image of God in
> humanity. Some sought it essentially in human
> rationality, others in dominion over creation, others
> in freedom of the will or moral qualities such as
> love or justice. . . . Yet it is important to insist that
> the whole person is the image of the whole, that is,
> the triune, God. . . . The incarnation of our Lord
> is definitive proof that humans, not angels, are
> created in the image of God, and that the human
> body is an essential component of that image.
> From the beginning creation was arranged, and
> human nature was immediately so created that it
> was amenable to, and fit for, the highest degree
> of conformity to God and for the most intimate
> indwelling of God.[1]

All of who you are is made in the image of all of who God is. Even though our image-bearing capacity is diminished by sin, it nonetheless remains.

Every single facet of what it means to be human is made to image God.

A person's capacity for logic and reason, another's physical strength, an athlete's hand-eye coordination, a friend's ability to intuit things, the grace with which your daughter moves, your manager's high emotional quotient, a designer's way with color, an author's proficiency with words, the way architects can envision things before they are built, the way geneticists understand the inner workings of things, the way your dad can hear when something is wrong, the way your mechanic loves to fix things, your neighbor's desire to serve behind the scenes, that teacher's ability to make the complex simple, that artist's yearning to create beauty, a disabled boy's ability to accept, a farmer's capacity to wait, an administrator's passion to put things in order, a mother's desire to bring life—all of these things image, in part, the God who made us.

God is perfect reason, strength, coordination, intuition, grace, emotion, aesthetics, voice, imagination, and understanding. He is the perfect discerner, repairer, server, clarifier, creator, accepter, adventurer, world-orderer, and life-giver.

God acts in all these ways, and when any of us do the same, we have an opportunity to simultaneously experience his presence built into us and surrounding us. There is a familiar knowing of God that can happen in the image-bearing process. As individuals we can know these image-bearing experiences only in part, because of sin and the fact that we've all been given different gifts. But collectively? Perhaps this is where we come closer to most fully bearing the image of God.

When people consider what they love about their jobs and what is "just right" about what they do—those moments of flow where work is life giving, good, and true—they often describe a resonant, image-bearing moment, a place where they are near God and where their work is in sync with God.

If Bavinck is right, if God did make us "amenable to, and fit for, the highest degree of conformity to God and for the most intimate indwelling of God," then surely every good unique facet of who we are and every "just right" Godlike action that we undertake, including those that play out at work, are imbued with revelatory potential.

That may sound like wishful thinking for those who aren't feeling a love for work right now, who took their job because it was the only one available, the only one they qualified for, or the one that their father or grandfather did. The thought of knowing God at work when work feels irrelevant, difficult, boring, and no more than the source of a paycheck must seem pretty distant. But it is precisely in these kinds of jobs that an experience of God at work can bring hope and meaning.

Consider the job of an electrician. Tough work. Hard on the hands. Often working out in the elements. At times dangerous. Surely a bit tedious once you've wired in your five hundredth wall receptacle. And still God is moving there.

What electricians love, I have learned, is energizing and enlivening things. They get excited by the light and power that they bring through their work. There is something about the moment when the lights first come on in a newly constructed building that is just right to them.

There's this feeling that "that was the final touch" that the room needed. You've got beautiful carpet,

paint, and finishes and now you've lit it up. It's one
of the most satisfying things to hit that switch and
see everything go, "Aaaaaaah!"

COREY ADAMS, MASTER ELECTRICIAN

I take tremendous satisfaction in turning on the
lights, but there's also great joy in hooking up big
motors or compressors or cranes. This unit just sits
there dormant until we hook it up and then it comes
to life. [The other day] we hooked up an overhead
crane—it's a beautiful system, an engineering feat,
and I applaud the engineers who designed it, but
until we get the wire and everything hooked up it's
just sitting there. And then when you test it and that
motor comes to life and it starts to move across the
beam. . . that's so cool! That's what I love.

ARNOLD DEES, MASTER ELECTRICIAN

These two electricians are made in the image of a God who
first spoke light and power into the universe.

In the beginning God created the heavens and
the earth. Now the earth was formless and empty,
darkness was over the surface of the deep, and the
Spirit of God was hovering over the waters.
　　And God said, "Let there be light," and there
was light. God saw that the light was good, and he
separated the light from the darkness. God called
the light "ON," and the darkness he called "OFF."

GENESIS 1:1-5 (SLIGHTLY PARAPHRASED)

When an electrician gets excited about the moment the lights come on or a machine first comes to life, in some sense they are imaging the joy God must have felt at the creation of the cosmos. When they experience that energizing delight, they are experiencing it in concert with their Maker—a real-time shared experience with God. Surely God delights in any activity that brightens his creation and enables it to become more fully perceptible and alive!

"GOD formed Man out of dirt from the ground and blew into his nostrils the breath of life. The Man came alive—a living soul!" (Genesis 2:7, MSG). This beautiful being—this bioengineering feat—came to life, started moving, and was now fully itself! God's energizing breath enabled a human being to flourish. God must have been overwhelmed with delight, a bit like how an electrician must feel when he first flips the switch: "Very good!" (1:31, MSG).

Philosopher Al Wolters explained humanity's cultural calling this way:

> The earth had been completely unformed and empty; in the. . . process of development God had formed it and filled it—but not completely. People must now carry on the work of development: by being fruitful they must fill it even more; by subduing it they must form it even more. . . . As God's representatives . . . [we] carry on where God left off. But this is now to be a *human* development of the earth. The human race will fill the earth with its own kind, and it will form the earth for its own kind.[2]

God is the source of all power and light. We are called to wire it in.

Commenting on Wolters's quote, Tim Keller writes, "It is [in] rearranging the raw material of God's creation in such a way that [work] helps the world in general, and people in particular, thrive and flourish."[3]

We are all called, through our image-bearing work, to help people thrive and flourish. The unique way that electricians do this is by building orderly connecting systems that enable an enlivening power to come to a not-yet-fully-itself device or place.

In this way, electricians are like the God who made a way for his Holy Spirit—his life-giving breath—to come into and enliven this world.

The Holy Spirit is God's power and energy, "the agency by which God gets things done."[4] The Spirit brings life and insulates us from the chaos. The Spirit empowers people with illumination, wisdom, spiritual gifts, creativity, skills, energy, movement, strength, and a sense of justice and truth. The Spirit brings order, begetting a world that is knowable— a world that our image-bearing reason can read, relate to, and understand so that we could discover electricity in the first place and then help humanity flourish by harnessing and stewarding it well.

Electricians are made in the image of a world-empowering God, one who makes a way for his mysterious, wild, and sometimes dangerous power to plug into and enliven us.

These truths change what an ordinary day on the construction site might look like for electricians. Every task they undertake in bringing that enlivening power has the potential to point to and offer an experience of their energy-supplying God.

What if electricians were cognizant of the *connecting* nature of their Maker every time they attached a wire to a panel or to a receptacle? The physical act of bending the wire and tightening the screw could then become a kind of embodied liturgy—a ritualized reenactment of a God who connects. And when a conduit is measured out, precisely bent, and installed in perfect parallel, the electrician may be mindful of a God who brings his power in a safe, at-just-the-right-angle, craftsmanlike way.

What is it about any craftsperson, working with her hands, that often feels so right? Did God make this artisan to know him via touch, via her hands? People who work in the trades often talk about how they love working with their hands and how it comes naturally to them.

And it should come naturally! God made those hands! He created our sense of touch as a means of engaging his revelation in a physical world. It is a different—but valid—way of knowing and worshiping.

If our whole being images God, then there must be a kind of communicating, listening, understanding, and knowing that comes through our hands, through our sense of touch. Touch is an embodied way of knowing that engages the truth by grounding us in reality and putting us in a specific place at a certain time. It conveys knowledge in a way that is uniquely sensitive to surrounding physical constraints. As one woodworker put it, "Without the opportunity to learn through the hands, the world remains abstract, and distant, and the passions for learning will not be engaged."[5]

AUTOMOTIVE MECHANICS

Automotive mechanics know exactly what this means. They know how to *know* through their hands. They know the precise amount of torque to put on a wrench in order to either safely unfasten a bolt or realize that the bolt is in trouble and seized up. When a mechanic sits in the front seat of your car and starts your out-of-tune engine, he can feel the problem through his hands and feet. When adjusting an old-school carburetor with a screwdriver, mechanics just know when they have found that in-tune sweet spot—when the engine is as it should be, when it is no longer falling short or missing the mark.

Automotive professionals bring mechanical renewal to our world through their hands.

In a way, every time they touch something they are recalling and reenacting the incarnation of Jesus Christ: the fact that he came to us and took on human flesh. Theologian Cornelius Plantinga Jr. observed that Jesus honored the trades when he "built the kingdom as a carpenter before he built it as a rabbi."[6] I think Jesus also honored our hands and God's good sensory gifts of touch, physical dexterity, and tacit physical knowledge.[7]

God's world-making power is revealed in the design of a human hand: in how it moves, feels, preaches, listens, witnesses, makes, and makes new. All of these capacities are held in God's sovereign hand.

God understands that there is a way of knowing that can come through and be expressed only by way of our physical hands. He is fully aware of and celebrates the implicit knowledge that is embodied in the appendages and mind of a tradesperson.

Jesus may have experienced this when he, as a builder, was faced with a complex construction challenge. As he stared down the problem, the solution would come to him out of nowhere; he would see what needed to be done in his mind, and then, moving with his hands and body, he would make it happen.

Jesus would know the God-given joy of an abstract idea or solution being translated into a concrete creation. Before anything in this universe even came to physically be, it was a thought in the mind of God—a thought in the mind of Jesus.[8]

When those who work in the trades work with their hands, they are imaging a God who was the originator when it came to moving from the abstract to the concrete. And just like them, God made this move in very material ways! Physicality, it seems, is of prime importance to the God who made the universe. A material world must be the best world through which to lavish his love upon his people and through which to self-reveal. Tradespeople image God when they physically make things or repair things.

> You're deeply rooted in him. You're well constructed upon him. You know your way around the faith.
> Now do what you've been taught. School's out; quit studying the subject and start *living* it! And let your living spill over into thanksgiving.
>
> COLOSSIANS 2:7, MSG

Jesus (God with us) worked with his hands.

It is difficult to fathom, isn't it? That the eternal, universe-conceiving, all-knowing almighty God worked as a builder; interacted with a mentor; got dirty on the job; had calluses; knew the frustrations of a hammer to the thumb; and dealt with nasty slivers, the waste of mismeasurement, stiff joints, and substandard construction materials. He went home for dinner exhausted, spent time with the family, read, studied his Bible, laughed, and told work stories.

Surely Jesus knew that all of the physicality he embodied was a gift from God his Father (one that he would take back to his Father one day). He must have looked at his hands and marveled. Carpentry might have been a very spiritual discipline for him—every move a rite, each thought a word from God, every action communion.

Every job has its own unique rites, actions, and forms of communion. For an electrician it works one way, for a carpenter another way; for you, in your job, it happens through your typing style, therapeutic touch, free-throw technique, concrete-finishing brushwork, or the way you handle a product.

There is a way of knowing God that's most natural to you—your vocational love language.

While Jesus lived only one human life, he knew that there are as many different ways that a person can know and experience God as there are people or languages spoken. I think every person, every job, every sphere of God's good creation has its own language, its own way.

Through what language do you relate to God best? What dialect does God speak to others through what you do? What would it mean to be a better interpreter of all of the vocational languages God speaks?

A few years ago, with great expectation, I read an article on the world's top Chinese-English interpreter, Andrew Dawrant. Dawrant has translated for presidents, prime ministers, and top corporate leaders. Was there something the world's top translator of one of the world's most difficult languages could teach me about what it means to interpret various vocational languages?

A few things struck me as I read the piece. Regarding the translator's motivation, Dawrant notes, "I've always been fascinated with the idea of being able to speak with 'others,' or 'the other,' to somehow transcend that barrier that divides us. . . . Somebody has to be there, who is very good at expressing ideas on behalf of those people who don't speak English or don't speak other languages."[9]

It is hard not to imagine this same motivation moving in the heart of Jesus. All that mattered to him was transcending the barrier that divides us from God. He was very good at expressing God's words in a language we could understand.

Jesus knew how crucial this interpreting role was. God was saying things, and he needed to translate these words through logical statements, creational parables, and loving actions.

God is saying things through our jobs, saying things we need to hear, saying things others need to understand.

Dawrant spoke of being up on the issues under discussion by those he is translating: "How will you know what is unspoken and what was expected to be said that was not said unless you went in fully informed and knowing the expectancies that preexisted around the meeting?"[10] This reminded me of how saturated our lives need to be with all that we can possibly know about who God is. Unless you are totally immersed in the Scriptures, praying and living out a God-loving life, you will have great difficulty getting the interpretation right. You will miss the context, the tone, and the nuance. Unless you know that God can speak to and through your body, what he is saying and doing through you may never dawn on you.

In relation to what actually goes on in a translator's head, Dawrant explains, "In essence it requires the brain to perform two tasks at once, speaking and listening in two different languages."[11] This is the quote I resonate with the most. There is something about the fullness and confusion of this description that rings true. It is like how a moment of epiphany is both mysterious and multifaceted. The place Dawrant describes reminds me of my Internet connection, fully open to the flow of information in both directions. It is a linguistic experience of things coming together, of unity; of the confluence of language; of listening and speaking, all at the same time.

If there is a person who knows how to discern multiple voices on multiple tracks, interacting with and relaying all of them, it is Andrew Dawrant. And if this translator can do this work for the "mere" goal of better transglobal communication, then shouldn't we strive to do the same in relation to hearing and translating God's multilingual creational/vocational words? Imagine developing your capacity to hear, speak, and interpret more of what God is saying to a world full of people who can't understand.

LECTIO VOCATIO

- If God can be known through your physical image bearing, what does *what you do best* say about who God is?

- If God's best way of speaking to us was to take on a body, how does your body enable you to most fully say what needs to be said and what God means to say through you?

LEANING INTO GOD'S SIGNATURE MOVES

LEARNING TO RECOGNIZE HIS PRESENCE EVERYWHERE

The whole creation is nothing but the visible curtain behind which radiates the exalted working of [God's] divine thinking.

ABRAHAM KUYPER, *WISDOM AND WONDER*

....

Philosophy professor Esther Meek wrote about the process of how we come to know others better:

> We attend to his or her ways, so that we can come to identify patterns—*signature moves*, I call them. What are distinctive, reliable, delightful ways that that person has of operating? . . . My theologian friend, Mike Williams, argues in *Far as the Curse Is Found: The Covenant Story of Redemption* (2005) that this approach of identifying patterns is how we should understand how the Old Testament promises Christ. God sets the pattern of redemption, with Noah, and then with the Exodus, so that when Jesus comes, we

FEATURED IN THIS CHAPTER:
- Florist
- Nephrologist
- Scientist

will recognize God's ways. Study God's ways as the relationship unfolds, not so you can predict the future, but so that you will recognize God when he shows up. Expect to be surprised, but also expect, if you have attended to him in love, to recognize him. The Bible is the unfolding drama of the covenant relationship between God and his people. When you read it, you attend carefully so that you get to know God, so that you will know his signature moves, so that you will experience them in your own life.[1]

Shortly after his resurrection Jesus caught up with two of his disciples who were traveling on the road to Emmaus. While he walked right beside them and even talked to them about his own life, death, and rumored resurrection, they were "kept from recognizing him"—until Jesus opened their eyes by showing them a few signature moves.

First, he spoke to them about how all that was written in the Old Testament about the Messiah pointed to a Jesus who was like the one they had known (and his disciples' hearts burned within them as they listened). Then he shared a meal with them and "took bread, gave thanks, broke it and began to give it to them" (Luke 24:30). As he reenacted this ritual of breaking bread, their eyes were opened (verses 13-35)!

This is the kind of experience we're all meant for: to recognize a resurrected Jesus who, by his Spirit, is walking, speaking, and serving right alongside us.

Years ago I led a workshop at Calvin College in Grand Rapids, Michigan, about the idea of experiencing Christ everywhere. After my talk, a preaching/Old Testament professor emeritus came up to me and said, "I think I see what you are doing. I've spent my entire life connecting the Jesus of the New Testament to the Jesus of the Old Testament. You are connecting the Jesus of the New Testament to the resurrected Jesus today."[2]

Ever since he spoke those words I've been dreaming of all the different ways that Christ is prefigured in the Old Testament and then trying to apply them in the context of recognizing Christ in our world today. Jesus, the perfect prophet, was recognizable in all that was true in words of the ancient prophets and can be glimpsed in the prophetic nature of the words of a journalist today. Jesus, the perfect High Priest, was foreshadowed through the Old Testament priesthood and can be recognized in the work of anyone working in mediation or advocacy today. Jesus, the eternal King, was "present" in all that was wise, good, and just in the lives and rule of the kings of old and can be witnessed in the just-right leadership, policies, and decisions of your local mayor.

In a way, even as Christ was mysteriously "hidden" in the Old Testament, so too is he "hidden" in creation today. A deeper knowledge of God's signature moves in the Bible can help prepare us to recognize his signature moves in the world.

In a book that explores the link between faith and science, Abraham Kuyper wrote the following:

> The whole creation is nothing but the visible curtain behind which radiates the exalted working of [God's] divine thinking. . . . So we can and must acknowledge and confess unconditionally that all of creation in its

origin, existence, and progress constitutes one rich, integrated revelation of what God in eternity thought and established in his decree.[3]

As we consider the idea of signature moves, perhaps Kuyper's idea can be broadened in its application. If God's thoughts are embedded in physical nature, could they also be embedded in human nature, the culture we create, the history we live out, and the work we do, even as these things are tainted by sin? Could the signature moves of human beings and the culture we create be understood in ways that are not merely illustrative or metaphorical? If God's thinking is embedded there, then in some sense these thoughts really are present-day parables.

Years ago, with the help of nephrologist Dr. Garth Mortis, I preached a message on the human kidney, an organ that maintains homeostasis in the body. It keeps the *good* going and the *bad* in check and allows your body to stay in balance, to be at equilibrium. It regulates the body's internal environment and tends to maintain a stable, constant condition. As I came to understand the nature of the kidney, what came to mind was the doctrine of common grace, as articulated by Louis Berkhof:

[God's Holy Spirit] restrains for the present the
deteriorating and devastating influence of sin . . .
and enables [people] to maintain a certain order
and decorum in their communal life, to do what is
outwardly good and right in their relations to each
other, and to develop the talents with which they
were endowed at creation.[4]

The Spirit holds back the *bad* and keeps the *good* going!

Even as the kidney does this balancing work for the human body, so too does Dr. Mortis bring homeostasis to the whole of a patient's life, via his deep knowledge of how the human body works (a wisdom-like signature move) and his great bedside manner (a compassionate signature move). Through this nephrologist's work, God brings these things to his patients' lives.

As you consider the kidney's signature moves alongside a nephrologist's signature moves, what does this tell you about how the Spirit is now holding your life? For most of us, our kidneys have been doing their thing for decades deep inside us, and we've been unaware of God's homeostatic revelation there.

Human beings are made to recognize God's signature moves in this world, "to pry loose from its shell, as it were, the thought of God that lies embedded and embodied in the creation, and to grasp it in such a way that from the creation they could reflect the thought which God embodied in that creation when he created it."[5]

Scientists do this (at least the first part) all the time: prying loose the truths embodied in creation. Going further, suppose you connect those truths (or any present-day signature move that you encounter) to God's ways in an Old Testament story, to a divine attribute embedded in a parable, or to a particular truth in a teaching of the apostle Paul. Who knows what kind of epiphany might occur!

Surely the *being* of God is not that far away from his thoughts.

When our image-bearing minds resonate with God's,

engaging physical nature or a cultural product of human nature, surely Jesus is near and surely these resonant moments can be an opportunity to personally commune with him.

This can happen in all kinds of ways. We know God through the embedded thought we "pry loose"; we know him in the realization of how our human nature mirrors his nature in that resonant moment; and we know him through the embodied activity of doing something with the truth we've discovered—creating new cultural products or taking our discoveries further.

This kind of revelatory moment can happen anywhere. C. S. Lewis said that "every created thing is, in its degree, an image of God, and the ordinate and faithful appreciation of that thing a clue which, truly followed, will lead back to Him."[6]

Every created thing: all that is good, true, and right in red-wood trees, black holes, seeds, human bodies, family systems, sports, the arts, and computer software. The piece of creation you work with and the way you work with it both have the potential to image God. There is something of the mind of God embedded there.

Often scientists will settle for experiencing God only through the categories of mystery, awe, beauty, and wonder. This isn't a bad thing! There is a lot to be in awe of. But imagine a scientist of faith moving beyond wonder and engaging the reasoning, data-creating mind of God. Instead of just experiencing God in a numinous way, they could experience him in a rational way as well. Perhaps, for the first time, their experience of faith and science might move beyond awe and wonder to a deeper or *totally other* kind of knowing—

a more methodological revelation from God, a more cognitive engagement with the empirical mind of God.

The experience could be transformative.

Every person in every job is meant to experience that epiphany in which their unique way of thinking falls into sync with God's. To feel, in that numinous or rational moment, a very clear sense of who they are, that they themselves were conceived by a Greater Mind, that their way of being was imprinted upon them by their Maker.

What would it take for you to open your mind to this possibility in relation to your job? What theological shifts would you have to make? What would you have to add to your vocational worldview? Or take away from it?

The first step may be submitting to the fact that creation really is filled with the thoughts of God, that you are meant to grasp those thoughts, that work is a place where that can happen, and that none of this can happen apart from God's Spirit illumining your way.

This submission requires a step of faith. "Sometimes we have to choose to trust someone in the absence of full understanding, and do what that person says, as far as we understand it, if we are ever going to come to deeper insight," wrote Esther Meek. "Knowing God isn't the only knowing that requires this; understanding the calculus professor does too! Obedience is an indwelling that invites the real."[7]

We are taught, mentored, and apprenticed in the work we do. We faithfully submit to someone who is above or ahead of us, who is more learned and experienced, who knows the way. In order to engage the thoughts of the God who put those people there, we need to look and listen beyond them and obediently submit to the God of all first thoughts and to identify patterns and signature moves.

For this process to play out in an effective way, we need to be *very familiar* with the God of the Bible. Without a deep knowledge of the God of the Scriptures (the Old Testament and the New) we won't be able to recognize his signature moves in creation.

We need to wear the Bible like a pair of glasses and let its truths bring clarity, context, and focus to our engagement with God's revelation in the world.[8] In the Bible, God's Word is closer, clearer, and more reliable. It has been exegeted, studied, and vetted for millennia. It is written down . . . in words!

The same goes for having a good grasp of theology and church tradition (as they help interpret the Bible). The more you know, the more you will recognize God's signature moves in the world.

Knowing what John Calvin once wrote about the unique role of each person of the Trinity in creation was crucial for me as I sought to unpack the *arranging* passions of a florist: "To the Father is attributed the beginning of action, the fountain and source of all things; to the Son, wisdom, counsel, and the *arrangement in action*, while the energy and efficacy of action is assigned to the Spirit."[9]

Jesus *is* the arranger of all things! He is the wisdom behind all things, the shaper and holder of everything. He is the one who sets things in place (roses, baby's breath, human lives). He knows the seasons and occasions of life; *what is needed when*; and what color, life experience, floral shape, size, or texture fits best.

How could I *not* imagine Jesus creating the universe in a florist-like way—arranging a galaxy here, a few black holes there, and nine planets around that one star—making it all out of nothing more than his imagination?

The more you know God through your Bible and the better you understand your theology, the more equipped you'll be to recognize God's signature moves.

LECTIO VOCATIO

When I meet with groups to try to discern God's signature moves in their jobs, I begin with these three questions:

1. What do you love about your job? What is just right about what you do? (Try to recall a working moment where you experienced meaning, flow, significance, awe, beauty, justice, or a deep sense of satisfaction.) Write it down.

2. Why does that experience matter so much to you? Think about it. How does it make you feel? What does it say about how you were made?

3. As you consider and unpack your vocational loves, be mindful of any scriptural or theological truths that come to mind. Do you notice any similarities or correlations between your story and the Bible's story?

As you engage these questions in your work, you may begin to see a connection between what you love at work and what God loves. Invariably, the good that you are passionate about—the true, the beautiful, the meaningful—is something God is passionate about. In fact, God is often the satiating end to which the truth, beauty, and meaning you are articulating is pointed.

PART TWO

WHAT IS A PARABLE, AND HOW IS WORK A PARABLE?

NOTICING GOD'S UNNOTICED PRESENCE

THE PARABLE OF SANITATION WORKERS

Christ has swept away the dust with which man's sinful limitations had covered up this world-order, and has made it glitter again in its original brilliancy.

ABRAHAM KUYPER, *LECTURES ON CALVINISM*

....

After that, he poured water into a basin and began to wash his disciples' feet, drying them with the towel that was wrapped around him.

JOHN 13:5

....

I love practicing the spiritual discipline of watching people work. Recently I've been setting aside time to observe food-court cleaning staff wipe down tables, sweep up scraps, sanitize trays, mop up spills, and empty trash bins.

Often the person doing the cleaning is an elderly man or woman in a uniform, working to ensure that some young family has a clean place to sit down and eat. They move slowly and steadily with their heads down and their eyes trained on the task, doing *behind-the-scenes* work right in front of me.

FEATURED IN THIS CHAPTER:
- Sanitation worker
- Sweeper
- Homemaker
- Cleaner

It is messy and thankless work. It must be difficult to stay motivated for an entire shift: customers standing over your shoulder, waiting for the table to open up; people leaving messes they'd never leave at home; a boss always wanting things done faster.

Yet it is important work. Imagine the food court without them.

There are many unseen workers who keep our world clean: city sanitation-department employees, hospital maintenance staff, sewage-treatment plant workers, school janitors, street sweepers, and homemakers. So much cleaning work going on behind the scenes—most of it unnoticed.

So I try to notice. I do it, in part, because all work matters to God and every worker belongs to him, but also because God is revealing himself through the cleaning work they do. These jobs are modern-day parables.

In her fascinating book on New York City's sanitation department, cultural anthropologist Robin Nagle wrote about how sanitation workers become invisible once they put their uniforms on.[1] The general public tends to look down on their work as dirty, mindless, and somehow *less* and therefore barely sees them. Yet what they do is critical for the health and well-being of our lives, homes, cities, and world. It wasn't that long ago that waste-borne diseases plagued our cities. Go back 150 years to any major urban center and breathe in the summer air. The fetid smells emanating from open dumps and sewers would have been overwhelming! And yet those who keep our world clean remain unnoticed and invisible to us. They are doing good work for our well-being, and we ignore them.

Commenting on one garbage collector with whom she worked at the sanitation department, Nagle noted, "I was . . . observing a man who could stare so blatantly [at those he served] because any potentially disapproving members of the public wouldn't notice him doing it."[2]

This makes me wonder how much God is staring at us. Here he is serving us in so many ways through the cleaning work of others—and we turn a blind eye, look the other way, despise, and reject him. We fail to recognize that he *made* that person who is cleaning up, driving that truck, or laboring at the city dump. We refuse to understand how integral a part he plays in all of the cleaning that happens in our world; we turn our backs on his lordship over all things. We are so busy worrying about feeding ourselves and getting our own work done that we fail to notice what God is saying through those who work around us.

Sanitation workers image a God who cleans and maintains his creation. Their work points to a central tenet of our Christian faith: that God is a God who cleans up our lives (justifies us through the humble, selfless, servant-like work of Christ) and then keeps them clean (maintains and sanctifies us via the ongoing work of the Holy Spirit).

God wants us to have clean and healthy lives. People who do the work of cleaning are evidence of this fact. Their work is a daily parable affirming the presence of our world-cleaning God.

Yet we go about our working lives as through he is not even there. We believe in a God who is sovereignly and providentially cleaning our world, and yet his presence is invisible, inaudible, and unimaginable to us. There is a kind of hypocrisy in this—not noticing him in the small, practical things.

> You have your heads in your Bibles constantly
> because you think you'll find eternal life there. But
> you miss the forest for the trees. These Scriptures are
> all about *me*! And here I am, standing right before
> you, and you aren't willing to receive from me the
> life you say you want.
> JESUS (JOHN 5:39-40, MSG)

We say that we want real life, that we want to know God more in all things; and yet we fail or are unable to see what he is already doing through the people and work and world he has surrounded us with.

After the Resurrection, Mary Magdalene initially didn't recognize Jesus; she thought he was the gardener.

We often miss seeing Jesus in his world. Which might be why Jesus spoke so many creation-based parables.

A PARABLE-SPEAKING GOD

When his disciples asked Jesus why he told all these stories he responded,

> You've been given insight into God's kingdom. You
> know how it works. Not everybody has this gift,
> this insight; it hasn't been given to them. Whenever
> someone has a ready heart for this, the insights
> and understandings flow freely. But if there is no

readiness, any trace of receptivity soon disappears.
That's why I tell stories: to create readiness, to nudge
the people toward receptive insight.

MATTHEW 13:11-13, MSG

Jesus used parables to "create readiness, to nudge people
toward receptive insight."[3] He told earthy, everyday, human
stories about seemingly ordinary things—agriculture, home
building, and business management—to help us get to the
truth about the nature of his Kingdom (that it mysteriously
fills the whole of our material world) and help us know him for
who he really is (that he mysteriously holds all of it together).

By communicating God's truth through these very earthly
means, it is as though Jesus is affirming both his lordship
over it all and creation's innate value—that it was made
through him. Jesus is offering us a pointer to the scope of
his Kingdom plan and saving work—that *all things* really are
going to be made new!

So to help us see things straight, Jesus chose to communicate the most profound truths of God through the most
ordinary parts of creation: through nature, through human
nature, and through all of the activities our human natures
engage in—including our work. Jesus taught eternal truths
through everyday stories about farmers, managers, vineyard
workers, and judges—jobs that we could already understand and relate to. He drew upon vocational truths that
he had already embedded into our world and upon relevant
vocational "words" that he had already set into play at creation. Parables work, in part, because of the work being done
in them.

Jesus continues to speak work-based parables today—
stories that we are a part of. The Kingdom of Heaven is like
a sanitation worker!

Right now Jesus *knows* that sanitation workers, cleaners,
sweepers, and homemakers belong to God and that the Spirit
is very much at work, saying something through the humble,
embodied, image-bearing nature of their work. God cleans.
He has cleaned us up, and he will one day fully clean all
things up.

Jesus sees it even if we don't.

But imagine if we could.

What if cleaners themselves were able to sense God's
authorial presence; hear God's voice as he speaks their lives;
and know him through the truth, beauty, and meaning of
the circumstances they find themselves in? The Kingdom of
Heaven is like that moment of flow you feel when you get
lost in a day of spring cleaning, like the deep satisfaction you
experience when all of the windows sparkle, and like the joy
you feel when the riverbank is pristine once more.

LIKE NEW

Sanitation workers image a God who cares about aesthetics
and human health, but they also image a God who *makes
room for the new*!

Robin Nagle noted, "If consumed goods can't be dis-
carded, the space they occupy remains full, and new goods
can't become part of a household."[4]

Concerns regarding consumption and excessive waste
aside, there is something innately good about work that takes

away the *unnecessary used* to make room for the *necessary new*. This needs to happen within our bodies, and it needs to happen within our homes, cities, and global economic systems. Things are going to break down and will need to be removed and replaced. There is a pace at which waste removal is good and right so that life can be properly maintained and can flourish.

God takes out the trash to make room for the new. He does this for our souls by removing sin, shame, and guilt through the work of grace, mercy, and forgiveness. And he does this for our physical lives by removing material waste, sewage, and noxious smells through the work of sanitation workers and cleaners.

In the book of Revelation, an ascended Jesus says, "See, I am making all things new! . . . These words are trustworthy and true" (Revelation 21:5, ISV).

Through his death and resurrection Jesus accomplished and is accomplishing this promise. On the cross he took out the trash. At the Resurrection he ushered in new clean life. Spiritually and physically, he makes room for this new life. Jesus didn't die just to save people's souls. He died to save their bodies, as well. He didn't take out the trash just so that human beings could be cleaned up. His intent was to one day clean up the entire cosmos.

This is the scope of the saving work that God effected through Christ via his death and resurrection. Our world-cleaning work is mysteriously woven into his greater work in order to accomplish these very material and cosmic ends. When a janitor physically mops up a mess, they *truly are* participating in the here-and-now "making new" work of Christ.

Their work, in a front-end kind of way, foreshadows and offers a foretaste of what will one day be done perfectly: all things clean and new. It's as though Jesus is affirming his ubiquitous world-renewing presence through the cleaning work janitors do, reminding us of what he's promised. Cleaners everywhere bear witness to his world-restoring heart every time something is made pristine again and its former glory is able to shine through. Of course this restoration is only temporal. Dirt and grime will accumulate again. The "making new" work of a cleaner can only go so far. But it is a pointer, a parable through which we can see a more eternal truth.

SO WHO IS CLEANING UP AGAIN?

This may all feel a little bit conflated—Jesus cleaning, cleaners cleaning, Jesus cleaning through cleaners. This conflation is intentional—not to confuse, but to acknowledge the mystery of the place where God's sovereign will and our human wills meet. It is a place where we all are meant to live, where Christ in me is reality in the fullest sense, where God's will *is* being done on earth as it is in heaven, and where we can't tell the difference between what is coming from our wills and what is coming from his—a vocational moment where we get a glimpse of the mystery of our final union with a world-cleansing Christ.

Jesus has been *cleaning up* and *keeping clean* his world since its inception, through all of the ways of nature, people, and protocols and historic hygienic improvements that have been implemented throughout history.

And in a very real sense, we have Jesus to thank for the

centuries-long development of urban sewer and wastewater management systems; for the present-day municipal services that so efficiently remove garbage from our homes; for our ever-improving recycling programs; for the development and implementation of zoning bylaws and urban plans that protect us from noxious industries; for roads, parks, and health departments; for local, national, and global hygiene standards; and for the hearts and minds and muscles of countless people who care about keeping our world clean.

God so loves this world that he wants *all of it* to be clean and made new.

In his book *Engaging God's World*, theologian Cornelius Plantinga offered a beautiful portrait of the universal scope of God's world-cleaning plan from a speech that politician and theologian Abraham Kuyper gave at Princeton in 1898: "A sixteenth-century plague," Plantinga wrote, "had ruined the Italian city of Milan, and Cardinal Borromeo had bravely stayed to feed and to pray for those who were dying. Kuyper admired Cardinal Borromeo's piety, but he admired John Calvin's even more."[5] Plantinga goes on to quote Kuyper:

> During the plague, which in the 16th century tormented Geneva, Calvin acted better and more wisely, for he not only cared incessantly for the spiritual needs of the sick, but at the same time introduced hitherto unsurpassed hygienic measures, whereby the ravages of the plague were arrested.[6]

God's plan is to make all things new, in every sense—including the introduction of "hitherto unsurpassed hygienic measures" such as well-engineered sewage-treatment plants, properly maintained trucks, machinery and pipes, scientifically supported hygiene protocols, and well-managed city plans.

Our work is part of a big plan! God wants us to know that the ordinary things we do foreshadow his making *all things* new. And he wants us to know that we can experience him in the process.

The scope of God's restoration is immense. And, of course, it's not we who implement that plan. In the Bible, a made-new world (the new Jerusalem) comes down out of heaven from God. This new world will be more than just clean—it will be fully restored to its original glory. It is this made-new glory that our good cleaning moments offer a foretaste of.

GOD'S CLEANUP PLAN

God is telling this world-restoring meta-parable right now. Your work, the part he has written for you, is a part of and a pointer to this larger cleanup plan. If you were to step back a little, you might be able to see him: the God who is standing right beside you as you do your job.

In the Bible, heaven on earth is described as a beautiful and pristine city with real city walls, homes, trees, and a river. It will be a place that is filled with people—people who work, make things, and eat things—and (I'm guessing) it will also have a just-right, environmentally balanced, perfectly recycling, ever-renewing, and well-swept way of cleaning and disposing of things that makes room for the new, for the ever-new, for the new-every-morning that God has for those who love him.

Your life and work are a part of *that* story—salvation history—as it providentially moves toward that final end.

LECTIO VOCATIO

1. Clean your work space; as you do, consider what new thing you might be making space for.

2. The next time you feel the joy of a completed cleaning project, think about God's joy in cleaning up people's lives.

3. Talk to someone whose job it is to clean up after someone else. How do they react to the suggestion that the work they do helps you understand God better?

Perhaps the very ordinary act of cleaning is a good place to start discerning the parable that is your job. It is simple. It matters (to you, others, and God). And it might be a perfect first step toward meeting the often-unnoticed, world-cleaning God at work.

THE ICONIC NATURE OF VOCATIONAL PARABLES

HOW REVERSING YOUR PERSPECTIVE CHANGES YOUR VOCATIONAL POINT OF VIEW

Similia similibus cognoscuntur: "like is known only by like."

GABRIEL BUNGE, *THE RUBLEV TRINITY*

Several years ago, a judge from our community told me what she loved about her work. "I love listening impartially," she said. "Giving someone a fair hearing is very meaningful to me. All people want is to be heard." I could sense God's presence just behind her, within her, and before her. I was encountering God's heart for justice *through* her. God was speaking through one of his most exquisite pieces of art: a living, breathing, working human being!

FEATURED IN THIS CHAPTER:
• Judge

Through the nature of this particular judge, I encountered more of God's just heart and more of his presence. This judge had a deep compassion for the disadvantaged and underrepresented, which reminded me of the Old Testament God, who is the helper of the widow and fatherless.

Later, when I met with other judges, I saw other aspects of God's just heart. One judge sat on the edge of his chair as he expressed his incredulity at criminal selfishness: "It's not fair that that person had their house broken into, feels so violated, feels fearful, has had their well-being taken from them, has been preyed upon by another member of society." It was as though I were sitting before the righteous indignation of God!

Another judge spoke about his preference for giving oral judgments: "If you can't speak your judgment directly to the people you are judging, then you better go back and rethink what you are doing. There have been times when I have had my notes together and I'm orally delivering my judgment, where I have made the very risky decision to change my judgment in midflight. As I'm going through it, and the courtroom is full, and I'm looking at people, I realize it's the wrong thing to do. And so I make changes."

I saw the God who chooses to make and maintain eye contact when he judges, who highly values relationship, and who knows that his judgment will be best when it is made while looking at us, by being present to us, by using words that we can understand, and by entering into our world and submitting to the risk of open court. This judge's oral-judgment risk-taking was one of the most loving and respectful things he could do; he imaged an incarnating God, and his office felt holy, as though the Spirit of God was there.

He was an icon.

HOW ICONS WORK

Throughout the history of the church, icons—typically special kinds of paintings—were understood by many to be a means by which the viewer could experience the presence of God.

That experience was not merely cognitive, subjective, aesthetic, impersonal, or superficial; you didn't just look *at* an icon, you looked *through* it and mystically entered into the presence of God. Icons were understood to be a means by which even the uneducated could think theologically.[1] Through the prayerful engagement of an icon, complex truths about God's nature could be visually entered into and explored—by anyone!

God still reveals himself in this way today. What he has historically done via iconic paintings in the church, he's also doing through all of his handiwork.

God is using a world filled with icons—as found in nature, human nature, and our cultural activities and products—as a means of reaching us in our present-day theological illiteracy with deep and profound truths about who he is. Perhaps God is even using our work in this iconic way. He has done it before through a prophet named Jeremiah, who heard the word of God through a potter at work.[2]

> This is the word that came to Jeremiah from the
> LORD: "Go down to the potter's house, and there I
> will give you my message." So I went down to the
> potter's house, and I saw him working at the wheel.
> But the pot he was shaping from the clay was marred
> in his hands; so the potter formed it into another
> pot, shaping it as seemed best to him.
>
> Then the word of the LORD came to me. He said,
> "Can I not do with you, Israel, as this potter does?"
> declares the LORD. "Like clay in the hand of the
> potter, so are you in my hand, Israel."
>
> JEREMIAH 18:1-6

God's word to Jeremiah came through a potter working at his wheel.

A deeper look into the nature of icons—examining Russian iconographer Andrei Rublev's *Holy Trinity*—might help kindle our imagination.

The story depicted in this famous icon begins in Genesis 18. The patriarch Abraham is visited by what initially appears to be three men but who are actually angels—one of them is later identified as "the LORD" (verse 17). Abraham offers hospitality to his guests, and during a meal the visitors tell Abraham about a son that will be born to him, affirming God's covenant promise to make Abraham the father of many nations and to be his God and the God of his descendants. This meal was a pivotal moment in the history of God's people. And so artists painted it.

Earlier iconic paintings of that scene reinforced the angelic nature of the three guests and also included both Abraham and his wife, Sarah, within their frame. But as iconic history unfolded and this story was repainted over and over again, Abraham and Sarah were dropped from the scene, and the mysterious angelic nature of the guests further developed. As time passed, the relationship between the three visitors deepened: their faces were turned toward one another and hand gestures were modified to signal conversation and interaction. In Rublev's iteration, the three seem wholly engaged with one another while at the same time looking at us, as though they are inviting us into the discussion.

Over time, iconographers began to understand this Genesis scene as an event that prefigured the Holy Trinity: three men, three angels, three persons of God—Father, Son, and

Holy Spirit. This depiction was never meant to be a graven image. These artists knew God could never be painted. Nor was it *just* a story about three men, or three angels, sitting down to a meal. It was an event that captured *all* of these meanings—three men prefiguring three angels prefiguring a triune God.

The Old Testament is filled with prophecies foreshadowing the person of Jesus Christ. For centuries, the deeper meaning of these complex texts was buried. But after meeting Jesus in the flesh, the New Testament writers were able to recall and engage their Old Testament Bibles with new eyes and rekindled imaginations. Once the Holy Spirit had loosened their perceptions, they uncovered many Christ references and connections. These writers would have certainly understood that the prophet Isaiah was referencing a specific person from *his* day when he spoke of a child who would be born, a son who would be given, a shoot that would branch out, and a servant who would suffer and then be a light for the nations; but they now knew he was also alluding to this Messiah Jesus who had come and lived among them.

Father Gabriel Bunge wrote one of the best books I have read on Rublev's *Holy Trinity*. This Benedictine monk has a deep understanding of iconic tradition. One of the things that intrigued me in reading *The Rublev Trinity* was how Bunge constantly interchanged his naming of the characters in this famous painting. At one point he used Trinitarian language—Father, Son, or Holy Spirit—and then he switched back to angels or men. These descriptors are used interchangeably, as though they are synonymous. By addressing the icon in this way, he affirmed the importance and integrity of the original story while still addressing its deeper, prophetic truth.

This is an important point to consider when engaging creation as an icon. The thing you are looking through—someone's job, a piece of art, or a mountain—is still fully what it is, even as it functions as a pointer to God. The judges I spoke to were still mere human beings—mortal legal professionals through whom deeper truths about God could be understood and experienced. These judges were fully who they were and were pointers to God at the same time.

Sometimes, when I talk about God's presence through a created thing, people think I'm being manipulative or diminishing that created thing—taking away its innate aesthetic value, integrity, or free will. Others respond in the opposite way, worried that I'm lowering God to the level of a human being or an earthly material thing. Yet if the Bible's prophecies and stories are any indication, God seems to have no problem making these kinds of multilayered iconic connections, entering into our human stories again and again.

To believe in a providential God who holds all human history is to necessarily accede to *something more* that is happening behind the scenes. The Holy Trinity is prefigured in three men; God's just heart is revealed through the passion of three judges; and God's presence is just behind, within, and before you. For thousands of years, iconographers have understood this multilayered, outside-of-time, mystical view of reality: that the God who is three-in-one can certainly be here-and-there, then-and-now, hidden-and-now-revealed.

This kind of foundational mind-set is needed when

searching for God's presence at work. You are doing all that you do at work—thinking, creating, planning, serving, deciding—and at the same time God is doing something as well. It is in the context of fully holding on to both realities that an icon operates. To diminish one or the other would be to undermine an icon's revelatory power.

One last thought on the history of icons: In the Orthodox Christian tradition, icons have always been understood as a viable and parallel means by which theological thinking and development was undertaken.[3] What spoken theology was for the ear (in the words of a sermon), painted theology was for the eye.[4] So even as Rublev's iconic predecessors slowly developed the theological understanding of a Trinitarian presence in the story of Abraham's visitors, so too a clearer depiction and understanding of God's revelation through your life and work may come only over time.

REVERSE PERSPECTIVE

Father Gabriel Bunge described a technique that Rublev used in painting the *Holy Trinity* called reverse perspective. A deeper understanding of this technique will help release the iconic potential of the work you do.

The first time I laid eyes on the icon of the *Holy Trinity*, I was confused. I felt sorry for those artists back then who had no idea how perspective worked. So much of the painting seemed out of proportion, askew and misshapen. I remember thinking that this painter really couldn't see straight. But then I read something from Father Bunge and realized that I was the one not seeing straight:

Icon painting makes use of its own principles.
It consciously submits to its own rules and thus
renounces much of what is essential for [worldly]
painting. So, it rejects what the world considers to
be the natural, or central perspective, which issues
from the standpoint of the beholder, and chooses
what can be considered the unartistic *reverse
perspective*, which forces the beholder to surrender
his own standpoint, his sense of distance. Likewise,
neither are shapes and objects illuminated from
outside, rather they have their own source of light
within themselves.[5]

This is the kind of perceptual transformation we all need
to make if we want to better see God's on-the-job presence.
We need to be shaken out of our "center of the universe"
perspective on ourselves. We need to be unsettled and to
have our perceptions challenged. We need to realize that we
are not the beholders—we are the beheld. God is not made
visible by our light; we are made visible by his. What we so
naturally consider the right and only perspective may, in fact,
be the opposite of God's perspective. John Calvin asserted
that we can see God in the world only as we wear the spec-
tacles of Scripture, but if *we're* the ones wearing the glasses,
then it's still all about our point of view. Perhaps we need
to reverse our perspective and see the Bible and creation as
windows through which God looks at us.

So what would it mean to look at your life and your job
in reverse perspective? The question is already problematic
because *we* can't do it. In fact, we need to move out of the

center. We need to become infinitely smaller, like a vanishing point.

God is the one who sees, who is at the center of everything, whose perception and viewpoint define reality. God doesn't fit into your life; you fit into his. You are part of his story. This way of engaging reality is very much the opposite of all that comes naturally to us and all that society teaches. We live in a world where we are the authors of our destinies. Everything is as we perceive it and make it to be.

In order to be freed from this very limiting perspective, we need to let go of our need for control. There is much more going on than meets our eye, than what our mere rational minds and mortal senses can perceive. *Up* may be *down*, and what appears small may loom large from God's perspective. Perhaps this is why Jesus taught that we need to be like a child. Only a child is open-minded enough to imagine and make room for something this new.

Can you imagine doing your job as though it all depends on you, while at the same time being part of this amazing, eternal Kingdom of Heaven story that God is narrating? Imagine how new it would feel to jump from reality-as-you-see-it into reality-as-God-sees-it and then back again.

Through reverse perspective you are able to see reality from God's point of view. When you give up your perspective, you gain perspective. When you lay it down, you find it. When you start to see yourself as the one being seen, God is closer and larger, more present and real.

When God is that close, everything changes. Even our perspective on the *nature* of revelation changes.

This is kind of unsettling. For most of my life I've thought that God reveals so that I (and others) can hear. But even that seems a little self-centered, doesn't it? What if revelation has an even higher purpose? What if we think we're hearing when we're really just overhearing?

IT'S NOT ABOUT YOU

There exists within the Godhead a self-giving, ever-flowing, other-centric love. The Father loves the Son, the Son humbly defers to the Father, and the Spirit serves Father and Son and is loved by both with an everlasting love. The triune God is the embodiment of communal fullness—peace, delight, and relational joy. God as Father, Son, and Holy Spirit is a community of eternal mutual adoration and selfless service—a community that communicates. Jesus didn't do anything apart from the will of his Father in heaven. The Spirit works in accordance with the will of Jesus and the Father. Each part of the Trinity listens.

This is the God who is moving in the world and at your work. When we talk about knowing God at work, it is this triune, ever communing and communicating, ever serving and loving God whom we are talking about.

What implications does this have for engaging your job iconically?

One implication is that much of what we will know and experience of God may not be directly aimed toward us. Perhaps knowing and experiencing God at work is more about getting caught up in the love that is being extended from Father to Son, overhearing words of wisdom being whispered by Jesus to the Spirit, or catching a glimpse of the eternal joy expressed by Father and Son as the Spirit mysteriously brings more and more of heaven to earth. This way of seeing reality takes us out of the center of the universe. The act of compassionately listening to a fellow worker may be the Holy Spirit's way of bringing glory to Jesus—the one through whom that fellow worker was made. Your God-imaging ability to read a person like a book—so that you can make a good judgment—may actually be Jesus' built-in way to glorify the Father, who left it to Jesus to shape and make you the way he did. Could it be that every good relational act that you undertake is actually a manifestation of the triune communal love of God?

If the nature of Father, Son, and Holy Spirit is always about the *other*, then it seems that who we are in our jobs should ultimately reflect this nature. Everything we do at work should be for the person next to us: our coworker, customer, or competitor. As we image God in this selfless way, we will become more like him and discover that the more we give to that other person, the more we receive. We will image the God who is fully himself as he gives more and more of himself away. And we will be drawn into ever-deeper communion with God.

Duke University's Dr. Norman Wirzba wrote that "mutual indwelling, the other-in-me and myself-in-another, is at the heart of true reality."[6] We image God best when we reflect his all-loving communal nature, both in serving the other and in receiving from them. "True life is lived *through* the gifts of others," wrote Wirzba.[7] "This means that relation rather than substance is constitutive of a thing's being."[8]

This is a very important truth to consider. You are not primarily what you accomplish at work, nor is your value based on the sum of your aptitudes and skills. Who you are is defined by how you selflessly and humbly relate—how you give, how you receive, and how you image the giving and receiving God. Talk about a reversal of perspective!

This is the kind of God who is looking at you and writing the story of your life. He doesn't want you to see and experience him from afar. He invites you right into the highly relational center of who he is—his eternal triune love.

And the truth is, God doesn't want his communal love reflected *just* in you. He wants entire companies, cities, countries, and everything that fills this cosmos to be likewise transformed. It is to this end that God is moving. This is the story he is writing.

LECTIO VOCATIO

Reversing your perspective is a hugely challenging thing to do. It will upend your entire worldview.

When sixteenth-century mathematician and astronomer Nicolaus Copernicus first formulated a model of our solar system that placed the sun and not the earth at its center, he started a revolution in physics, philosophy, and faith.

Imagine having to admit that all you have ever known about the nature of reality was wrong. The sun doesn't orbit around you! You orbit around it! God isn't a part of *your* life. You are a part of *his*!

Even as Copernicus's findings are so obvious to us now, I wonder if, one day, we will feel the same about the true nature of our reality—that we really are invited into the intimate community of God.

In his *On the Revolutions of the Heavenly Spheres* (1543), Copernicus made this prescient observation as part of the list of assumptions that he based his theory on: "The distance from the Earth to the Sun is imperceptible in comparison with the height of the firmament [the rest of the universe]."[9]

These are the orders of magnitude we need to keep in mind as we consider the implications of a reversed perspective.

We are the negligible: called into relationship with the ineffable.

You are one human being, living an infinitesimally small life on one tiny planet orbiting a small star, which is one of hundreds of billions of stars that make up a galaxy that in turn is one of billions of galaxies that fill a universe held by an infinite God.

When you look up at the night sky, let the universe be your mentor.

When I consider your heavens,
    the work of your fingers,
the moon and the stars,
    which you have set in place,
what is mankind that you are mindful of them,
    human beings that you care for them?

PSALM 8:3-4

PART THREE

WHAT DOES GOD REVEAL TO US ABOUT HIMSELF THROUGH OUR WORK?

6

GOD MADE ALL THINGS (CREATION)

HOW GOD SPEAKS THROUGH YOUR JOB AND THE WORLD YOU WORK IN

Geophysics allows us to see things we can't see.

GEOPHYSICIST LEE WAMSTEEKER

....

In the beginning God created rock—a whole lot of rock, all kinds of rock, 5.97219×10^{21} metric tons[1] of rock for planet Earth alone. Igneous, sedimentary, and metamorphic; granite, limestone, and marble—God came up with them all. He conceived of the chemical bonds that would hold them together. He had a clear sense of how time would impact their formation. And for all we know, he loved looking at all of the rock he made, holding it in his hand like a delighted child with a newfound treasure.

FEATURED IN THIS CHAPTER:
- Geophysicist

God made this material world. And God loves it as a geologist or geophysicist loves it.

And the rocks, which God made, cry out.

Rocks say something about who God is, even as the God-imaging passions of geologists and geophysicists do. Even as the passions of any of us who work with the material elements that make up our world do.

God made us with passions and loves that reflect his passion and love. And he made us this way for a reason (for lots of reasons, I would imagine), the greatest of which would be so that we could know him more: through our love of rocks and trees and skies and seas and everything else that is. We can know him more as we explore *all* that he has made.

There is a *way* that things work in this world, a wisdom that God has woven into the created order, a *way* that points to the Way.

DISCOVERING GOD'S PRESENCE

One of the best parts of my job is meeting with small groups of workers from any given field to learn about their jobs as they better discern God's active presence at work. This collective effort is not only an effective way for *them* to discover God's on-the-job presence; it is also a means through which everyone in our community can do the same.

Discovering God at work can often be an epiphany. For some, it is the first time they have ever connected what they do on Sunday to what they do during the week. They have never imagined God actively working through them on the job. When they realize that they can know God through their unique passions and abilities, their experience of work is transformed. Their jobs become more God-aware, and this epiphany has led to a profound sense of delight and gratitude.

This happened to two geophysicists when we met. When

I directly connected the science of their field to their faith, the results were earthshaking! God became more real and present in the rocks they studied and in that place where they spent forty to fifty hours a week.

LEARNING FROM A GEOPHYSICIST

Geophysicists are good at naming an unseen reality. They can look at something as seemingly inert as rock and see movement—a story that has played out over time. They can even discern what lies beneath the surface of the earth: precious elements and resources that can help humanity flourish.[2]

The science of geophysics—using God's good gifts of seismic methodology and physical constants—helps a geophysicist contemplate who *Jesus* is through the world he made. By understanding the ancient and forever nature of rocks, something of Christ's *Alpha and Omega* nature can be known. As geophysicists recognize their God-given, God-imaging desire to peer into and explore the physical world, their knowledge and discoveries give them more geophysical truth to know and love God with.

Through the work of a geophysicist we can all learn how to see unseen things more clearly: via the nature of their method (the use of analogues), the object of their explorations (rock), and the image-bearing passions they embody. Each of these elements is part of the parable that makes up a geophysicist—God reveals himself to us through them and they co-illumine one another.

ANALOGUES

The job of a geophysicist is to interpret subterranean data and determine the specific nature of what is buried or concealed (often in the search for mineral, oil, or gas deposits). One way they do this work is through the use of *analogues.*

In order to "read" a reef two miles down, you must first look at how reefs are shaped in oceans today (geophysicists actually go on diving expeditions as on-the-job training). To discern the makeup of an ancient subterranean mountain that you will never be able to physically see, you need to look at a mountain that you *can* see.

Geophysicists use knowable data as an analogical lens through which to "see" the unseeable.

The moment I heard about analogues, the theological concept of anthropomorphisms came to mind. It is a technique used in the Bible where writers take human attributes (hands, eyes, feet, face, language) and emotions (anger, love, patience) and use them to help describe a concealed or unseeable God. They use knowable data as a lens through which we "see" the unseeable.

We see this in the very human language God uses as he speaks to Moses in this passage from the book of Exodus: "When my glory passes by, I will put you in a cleft in the rock and cover you with my *hand* until I have passed by. Then I will remove my *hand* and you will see my *back*; but my *face* must not be seen" (Exodus 33:22-23, emphasis added). An omnipresent God doesn't have a physical body—no hands, no back, and no face. And yet God uses this very down-to-earth language as a means for us to perceive him—as a way for the finite to grasp the infinite. God uses the image of a hand to reach out to us; through the expression of a face, he looks upon us, listens, and speaks. "According to John Calvin, because God chose to reveal himself to finite—and, after the fall, sinful—people as a holy, eternal being, he had to accommodate himself to human language, emotions and objects. The Bible leaves no doubt that these anthropomorphic self disclosures are forms of genuine self revelation."[3]

God uses earthly things to help us know and experience him; he goes so far as to take on a human body (with hands, a back, and a face) in the person of Jesus Christ in order to make himself clear!

Admittedly, the analogues and anthropomorphisms we humans come up with fall short. God's love is *like* a father's, but an earthly father can never perfectly express the fullness of God's heart. A present-day reef may be *like* an ancient Devonian reef, but it won't be exactly the same. The mystery of God's timeless nature might become more fathomable when understood in the context of geological time, but even a 4.5-billion-year-old planet can't come close to capturing the true scope of his eternality.

There is an art in applying and interpreting both anthropomorphism and analogue. These methods aren't perfect, but there is certainly something of the unseen that can be seen and known via these analogical/anthropomorphic methods. Subterranean geological formations can be known to a degree via analogy, and God can be known in part via anthropomorphism. And these "knowings" are similar. Perhaps more so than we have ever imagined!

KNOWING GOD THROUGH ROCK

It is compelling to consider that God's truth in geophysics—the use of analogues as a means for seeing the unseen—could help us better see an unseen God, and that the way of analogues could inform, enhance, and help us further unpack how God uses human traits (anthropomorphisms) to self-reveal.

Consider further that a geophysicist's methodology might actually expand the scope of the means by which God self-reveals: from using *just* human attributes and relational characteristics to also using geological materials and categories such as reefs, mountains, and the science of seismic physics. That opens up a whole new world of divine revelation!

God really does speak through rocks. God is self-revealing through both organic and inorganic realities, via both relational and material categories, via both words and world.

The very physically engaged jobs that many of us do are a means through which we are called to listen to and discover a God who is speaking everywhere, through all things. An astronomer discovers God in star-birthing galaxies, a farmer in the fertile nature of soil, a mechanic in the engineered brilliance of machines, a midwife in the miraculous power of the birthing process, a writer in the mystery-revealing nature of metaphor, and a server in the selfless gift of hospitality.

Our jobs, and the material realities that they engage, are a hands-on way of knowing God through his world—an embodied, thoughtful, sweating, struggling, challenging, and creative way of living into and experiencing his materially imaged presence.

Theologian Herman Bavinck would agree:

Revelation, while having its centre in the Person
of Jesus Christ, in its periphery extends to the
uttermost ends of creation. It does not stand isolated
in nature and history, does not resemble an island
in the ocean, nor a drop of oil upon water. With the
whole of nature, with the whole of history, with the
whole of humanity, with the family and society, with
science and art it is intimately connected.

The world itself rests on revelation; revelation is
the presupposition, the foundation, the secret of all
that exists in all its forms.

That is a pretty all-encompassing view of how and where
God speaks. Bavinck goes on:

The deeper science pushes its investigations, the
more clearly it will discover that revelation underlies
all created being. In every moment of time beats the
pulse of eternity; every point in space is filled with
the omnipresence of God; the finite is supported by
the infinite, all becoming is rooted in being.

And then Bavinck draws the person of Jesus into his cosmic
revelatory vision:

Together with all created things, that special
revelation that comes to us in the Person of Christ
is built on these presuppositions. The foundations
of creation and redemption are the same. The Logos
who became flesh is the same by whom all things

were made. The first-born from the dead is also the first-born of every creature. The Son, whom the Father made heir of all things, is the same by whom he also made the worlds.

After affirming the supremacy of biblical revelation, Bavinck goes on to speak about the nature of the relationship between creational (general) revelation and biblical (special) revelation:

General revelation leads to special, special revelation points back to general. The one *calls for the other*, and without it remains imperfect and unintelligible. *Together* they proclaim the manifold wisdom which God has displayed in creation and redemption.[4]

This is the way God's revelation works: two books, one Author. The Bible and the rest of the created order together, co-illumining one another. The part of creation you engage via your work is something through which God speaks. The way that you engage that creational thing is a pointer to God's ways.

Think about how the concepts of analogy and anthropomorphism work. They connect two realities that are separated by time and space—one closer to you and more knowable, and one far away and less knowable. The more knowable reality sheds light on the less knowable, giving you a better understanding of that reality. When the two texts of a modern-day reef and an ancient reef talk, greater truth is revealed.

The analogical method that is so ingrained in geophysics is meant, by God, to be a way through which geoscientists can study, know, and experience him more. Perhaps all of what makes up creation and all the ways of exploring creation are meant to be used to this end. Everything in the cosmos is meant to bring God glory: the nature of metal and the metalworker, emotions and the psychologist who studies them, flowers and the florist who arranges them.

You, the job you do, and what you work with are all part of a world that God made. God is the originator of the science that makes up geophysics. He created a universe based on physics. He made it (in part) for you.

GEOPHYSICAL PROVIDENCE AND STEWARDSHIP

God created this planet so that we could have a home. God hospitably placed subterranean gifts within the earth to aid in our sustenance and flourishing: precious metals, minerals, and even the gift of fossil fuels. God then provided uniquely impassioned individuals to help locate and retrieve those gifts. Geophysicists see that God cares about keeping humanity moving and warm (in the case of buried energy), so much so that he thought to make preparations millions of years ago.

That may sound a bit naive, given the environmental state of our overheating planet. But it's an important point to make. Just because we have severely messed up in our pursuit of and use of the world's natural resources doesn't mean that the use of the resource itself is the problem. Like all good things in creation, natural resources can be—and are—misused. But to say that the extraction of these non-renewable resources is, in and of itself, to blame for the environmental mess we're in is like blaming painkillers for society's addiction problems. There is a right way and a wrong way to use all of God's good creational gifts. We must be careful not to let the brokenness of a thing mask its innate and original creational goodness.

Sometimes I wonder whether we'd steward nonrenewable natural resources better if we perceived them as a gift, revealing something about the nature of a providential God. That God would put so much forethought into making a world with all of this built-in energy and resource can inspire us to treat what he's made as a very precious resource. God has given us an amazing gift to be used with reverence and to be rightly researched and understood, so that we can grasp the implications of its life cycle use and not disrupt those miraculous rock formations any more than we have to.

If we experience our natural resources in a revelatory way, knowing God through what he's made, our hearts and minds will be changed. We will better image God: loving the creation he made, having respect for its incredible intricacies, and making better ethical and environmental choices. We'll reflect his "best practicing" heart. We'll do unto others as we would want them to do unto us. If we know God more through his creational gift, we'll be changed for the better.

Or not. We can choose to *not* listen to God's subterranean revelation and not make the best choices.

A GEOPHYSICIST'S IMAGE-BEARING PASSION

Our jobs belong to God, and they are a means through which we can know and experience him. The science, the inherited knowledge, the traditions or cultural practices, the creativity and ingenuity, the physical prowess, and the willpower that we work with every day all belong to God.

Imagine what a geophysicist could come to understand about God over the course of a lifetime's work! Every time she put her hands on a new data set, the questions would return: *What will this teach me about how to see you more, God? How will I see your face in these ancient geological forms this time around?*

Even as the New Testament's authors were able to mine and discover the mysteries of Christ buried in the Old Testament texts, geophysicists today help us discover Christ—the one through whom God made the universe (see Hebrews 1:2)— through our planet's ancient geological forms.

Writer Marilynne Robinson, commenting on John Calvin's thought on the nature of humanity, offers some helpful perspective:

> [Calvin] places this incandescent divinity—it is
> the glory of God that "shines forth" from human
> nature—at the very center of individual experience
> and presence. And this sacredness is an attribute not
> of saints only, nor of Christians only, but is inherent
> and also manifest in all human beings as such.[5]

Through a geophysicist's image-bearing glory, God's glory is revealed. Through the ordering of her mind, the ordering mind of Christ can be seen. The geophysicist and the geophysics with which she works become icons, things we can look *through* to encounter the presence of Christ—the one through whom all things were made (John 1), the one in whom all things hold together (Colossians 1), the one for whom all things were made (Colossians 1), the one who is making all things new (Revelation 21).

> Who, after all, made the world of nature, and then made possible the development of sciences through which we find out more about nature? Who formed the universe of human interactions, and so provided the raw material for politics, economics, sociology, and history? Who is the source of harmony, form, and narrative pattern, and so lies behind all artistic and literary possibilities? Who created the human mind in such a way that it could grasp the endless realities of nature, of human interactions, of beauty, and so made possible the theories of such matters by philosophers and psychologists? Who, moment by moment, sustains the natural world, the world of human interactions, and the harmonies of existence? Who, moment by moment, maintains the connections between what is in our minds and what is in the world beyond our minds? The answer in every case is the same—God did it. And God does it.[6]

One of the geophysicists I spoke with said that what he loved most about his work was how it enabled him to see that "creation was still happening." By spending a big chunk of his cognitive life two miles down and 200 million years ago, he was able to realize that hundreds of millions of years from now, the earth's surface as we know it may, in fact, be two miles beneath the surface.

Physical creation is still happening. God continues to make more with what he has made. Theologian Jan Veenhof agrees: "Creation is not just a past event but a continuous process. God remains Creator up to the present day."[7]

God is the creator right now. God is creating culture and society right now. God is working through all kinds of workers in order to do his creating work right now.

God is working through you—right now.

And you are meant to and created to appreciate that.

LECTIO VOCATIO

- Take an inventory of the "stuff" you work with (numbers, children, words, food, etc.). What do you work with most?

- How do the visible things you work with reveal the unseen presence and nature of God? What does their shape, sound, nature, age, feel, color, beauty, goodness, strength, name, or significance say about what God is like?

- How does God's revelation through the things you work with resonate with his revelation through the parable that is your job? Take note of where you see synergies or co-illumination.

- Try to recall whether the stuff you work with is ever mentioned in the Bible (bread, wine, saving actions, acts of hospitality, parties and feasts, poetry, rocks and trees, etc.). God used these created things in the Bible. How is he using those same things now?

After preaching on God's truth in geophysics, I received a short note from one of my fellow sermon researchers: "I'm so thankful to have had the opportunity to work with you on this. It has really made a difference in the way I look at my work. I have a feeling that it will really hit me tomorrow morning when I log in to my computer at the office. Geophysics, for me, has been made new again!"

SIN DISTORTS ALL THINGS (FALL)

HOW PRIDE, GREED, GLUTTONY, ANGER, SLOTH, LUST, AND ENVY KEEP US FROM EXPERIENCING GOD AT WORK

In their pride the wicked do not seek him; in all their thoughts there is no room for God.

PSALM 10:4, TNIV

....

In 2009, New York lawyer Marc Dreier was sentenced to twenty years in prison for securities fraud, wire fraud, and money laundering. He had set up a Ponzi scheme and stolen hundreds of millions of dollars from investors. He did it because he desperately wanted to be the kind of person who mattered, who was successful and respected. Instead he lost himself.

FEATURED IN THIS CHAPTER:
• Crooked lawyer
• Immoral federal politician
• Accountant

In the 2011 documentary *Unraveled*, based on Dreier's story, there are several scenes where the director's camera is tightly trained on Dreier's face. He is awaiting sentencing and isn't denying any of the facts regarding what he did. But during these uneasy, intimate moments, it is clear that this brilliant man hasn't come fully clean; he cannot see his broken nature for what it is. You, the viewer, find yourself feeling incredulous at his denial. How can he not see it? How can he be so unaware? It is the kind of incredulity that God must often feel when he looks upon each of us.

Like Dreier, we all are prone to deny the facts when it comes to our sinful culpability. We defend ourselves with stories of people who behave worse than we do in order to hide from the truth. We focus on the good things we have accomplished in an attempt to create a smoke screen. We hide behind lies and tell ourselves that this is the way business works, everyone cuts corners, we deserve this. And then, at the end of the day, we launder our guilt by giving some of our ill-gotten gains away.

The Bible—in addition to the witness of history—teaches that everyone sins and falls short of the glory of God. This is irrefutable. No human being has ever disproven the fact. We are created with so much potential for good and yet are tainted with a fatal propensity to fall short; miss the mark; and act in corrupting, perverting, and polluting ways.[1]

To the extent that we are this way—and that we exacerbate the effects of this reality via our denial—we undermine our capacity to know and experience God. An Old Testament psalmist wrote, "If I had cherished sin in my heart, the Lord would not have listened" (Psalm 66:18). Sin interferes with and impedes communion with God—in two directions. It causes God not to listen, and it leaves us unable to hear. This has huge implications for knowing and experiencing God, especially in the workplace.

Is there a way that the communication-muting effects of sin can be countered or undone? The answer can only come as the full scope and nature of the problem of sin is exposed.

To get a better grasp of how sin works and how it limits our capacity to experience God in the workplace, we will look at the infamous seven deadly sins—pride, greed, gluttony, anger, sloth, lust, and envy.

PRIDE

When I first read about pride in C. S. Lewis's *Mere Christianity*, I was undone. At the time, I was working as the director of development on a large real-estate project, and I was very full of myself. Only I didn't know it. I had the suit, the office, the car, the decision-making authority, and a huge ego. I read Lewis's words describing the kind of person for whom pride was the biggest problem: "If you think you are not conceited, it means you are very conceited indeed."[2]

I was stopped in my tracks. "What? Me?" I knew a lot of guys with big pride problems. They drove me nuts. But I wasn't like them. Lewis went on, "There is one vice of which no man in the world is free; which every one in the world loathes when he sees it in someone else; and of which hardly any people . . . ever imagine that they are guilty themselves."[3]

I was busted. And ever since, I have been plumbing the depths of pride's sinful grip in my life.

Pride can be described as

> inordinate self-centredness, self-absorption, and self-esteem. It's the self, filled with self and is most often born out of insecurity. Unlike some of the other deadly sins, pride stands alone. While greed, lust, gluttony, sloth, envy and anger can bring people

together, pride doesn't. By definition it divides, separates, it is enmity.[4]

Now that is dark and deadly! And it is alive and well in you, hidden in that blind spot you don't know is there. And it is keeping you from God. If your self is filled with self as you manage others, work with patients, or build that house, how can you ever have room for God? As C. S. Lewis wrote, "A proud [person] is always looking down on things and people; and, of course, as long as you are looking down, you cannot see something that is above you."[5] Lewis is affirming the wisdom of the psalmist: "In their pride the wicked do not seek him; in all their thoughts there is no room for God" (Psalm 10:4, TNIV).

If you want to meet God at work (or anywhere else), you need to find your place in his grand story. You will never discover where you fit in if you are too big for the part. Pride blinds you to yourself. When you spend all your energies worrying about how you are perceived, you are reducing your capacity to discern how God is seeing you and working through you. Faculties of perception that are meant to be trained on a *God who sees you* are being misappropriated for selfish means—so that *you can see you*. Instead of seeing your innate entrepreneurial gift—the ability to create something out of seemingly nothing or to imaginatively see a connection where no one else can—as a God-given quality with which you can humbly experience *his* image-bearing power in you, you make it all about you! Instead of entering into God's glory, you fill yourself with your glory. And if you are really full of it and pride has completely taken over, you don't even worry about what God or the rest of the people in the room are thinking.

In his book *Pride*, Michael Eric Dyson writes that we need to realize that other people are *not less* than we are (in fact they are more). They deserve to be seen, heard, and respected. They are there. They are worth it. And they demand (in the best sense of the word) your proper attention. Your world would be less without them—the *whole* world would be less.

These people have huge hopes for their lives. They possess great God-given potential . . . to live and be and have their being! Each of their lives is a story that is part of an even bigger story: God's story. They are not there simply to build you up. They deserve your delight.[6]

This kind of humility images God's heart, and practicing this selflessness will bring you closer to him. That nearness will protect you from yourself; it can't ever be all about you when you know that God is standing right there.

GREED AND GLUTTONY

Greed and gluttony are both appetite disorders. "Greed," Henry Fairlie wrote, "is the excessive and insatiable appetite for wealth and possessions. It loves not possessions so much as possessing."[7] Gluttony is "the willful and insatiable desire to overconsume, excessively elevate, and be preoccupied with that which God created for good. It is more interested in consuming than in what is being consumed."[8] Both infect our desires and, if left unchecked, can leave us in a state of perpetual dissatisfaction. One researcher bluntly stated that consumer culture offers "an infinite propagation and replication of 'desire' that feeds on itself and has no outside and no fulfillment."[9]

The desire for more is not in and of itself sinful. Wanting a fulfilling job, higher pay, better working conditions, greater autonomy, work that allows you to master your craft and make a contribution—these are all good yearnings![10] Where greed and gluttony cause a problem is when these good desires are allowed to freely manifest in unregulated ways. Then life and work become *all about* consuming and possessing. Soon our lives are characterized by what sociologist Peter Corrigan describes as "the need to need, the desire to desire."[11]

Greed and gluttony take strong, God-given passions and corrupt them, artificially stimulate them, unbridle them, and then set them off in the wrong direction. No sooner do you receive a pay raise or bonus than you fixate on the next increase, the next promotion, the next company. You spend more than you can afford in order to dress the part, drive the right vehicle, eat at the right restaurants, and post the right holiday pictures. You spend so much time and attention looking around and ahead, always measuring and comparing, that you never really get a chance to rest in your job, delight in what you have, and consider the God who gave it all to you. Thomas Aquinas describes five different ways that gluttony leads us to overindulge: We consume too soon, too eagerly, too much, too expensively, and with too much fuss and attention. While we certainly do this with food, it appears that we also do it with our careers.

So how do we dial back greed and gluttony at work? Ironically, it starts with affirming the insatiability of our desires. As theologian Lesslie Newbigin said, "Because man is so made that only God can satisfy him, his desires are unlimited."[12] What greed and gluttony take advantage of is arguably one of the strongest forces in human nature. We are meant to never get to the "end" of God. He is infinite and eternal, and he has therefore given us unlimited desires. God is the one whom we are meant to consume—now, eagerly, more and more, richly, and with our fullest attention. This is what our insatiable desires are made for.

How many times must we read about the destructive stories of greed gone wild—bloated overconsumers unable to move; aspiring workers getting to the top and realizing that there is nothing there; human beings, in ever increasing ways, being commodified, dehumanized, impersonally identified by their net worth, or described as being mere human resources—before we get it? And what about all of those souls who are left behind by our greedy pursuits, stuck on that lowest ladder rung, unable to make more than the minimum wage all because the biggest pieces of pie have already been eaten? You are made in the image of a God who flourishes when others flourish,[13] so how does taking more than your share image him?

> What I'm trying to do here is get you to relax, not be so preoccupied with *getting* so you can respond to God's *giving*. People who don't know God and the way he works fuss over these things, but you know both God and how he works. Steep yourself in God-reality, God-initiative, God-provisions. You'll find all your everyday human concerns will be met. Don't be afraid of missing out. You're my dearest friends! The Father wants to give you the very kingdom itself.

Be generous. Give to the poor. Get yourselves a
bank that can't go bankrupt, a bank in heaven far
from bankrobbers, safe from embezzlers, a bank you
can bank on. It's obvious, isn't it? The place where
your treasure is, is the place you will most want to
be, and end up being.

JESUS (LUKE 12:29-34, MSG)

ANGER

But what if things are genuinely broken at work? Your boss is
abusive. Safety codes are being violated. You have been passed
over for that promotion twice. The company lost the contract.
Half of your department has just been laid off. The patient
died. Your coworker threw you under the bus. The project fell
apart. You have just been let go.

Surely anger is an appropriate response to injustices like
these.

Anger, rightly felt and expressed, is not a sin (Ephesians 4:26).
But we need to be careful that our anger isn't expressed in an
inappropriate way—like putting so much pressure on an elec-
trical engineer that he ends up having a mental breakdown, or
abusively making the contractor pay for his mistake no matter what the extenuating circumstance, or leaving an on-site
meeting in a huff when a consultant is a mere five minutes late
(I still feel guilty about these incidents).

Anger that is culpable is "a *vengeful* or *destructive* passion,
often *uncontrolled*, that flares up against a person or thing
giving pain or frustration. This passion can be exhibited
outwardly via an outburst or swallowed yielding resentment

and potential bitterness."[14] When anger at injustice becomes vengeful, then you are ignoring the God who said, "Vengeance is mine" (Romans 12:19, ESV). When you destroy a coworker with your words or actions, face to face or behind their back, you are ripping apart an individual whom God loves. When you fly off the handle in an out-of-control rage, you are not imaging a God who is patient, who doesn't dishonor others, who is not self-seeking or easily angered, and who keeps no record of wrongs (1 Corinthians 13:4-5).

If you are in sync with God's will for the parable that is your job, your anger will be under control. If it is out of control, you can be assured that you are too far from God to hear, see, or know him. Out-of-control anger can create so much psychological and spiritual interference (via its expression or by swallowing it) that you are almost guaranteed to lose sight of God's presence in your workplace.

Knowing that God can handle things can help you lengthen your fuse and keep you from unhealthily swallowing your rage. Having left vengeance in heaven's lap, you might be able to seek mediation or justice with a tempered heart. Perhaps then the offending party will be able to hear your grievance in a restorative way. And you will be more patient, honoring, measured, controlled, and in the best place to be forgiving—which is the *ultimate* antidote for anger. Being close to a God who forgives you may help you to do the same.

Another antidote to anger would be to let go of perfectionism, which may be the single greatest cause of anger and frustration at work.[15] The Bible teaches that human beings once lived in a state of perfection and will one day live in that place again. But right now we are not there. A lot of our anger is born out of the frustration we feel when unreal expectations aren't met. We put ourselves down for not being perfect or getting it right the first time. Instead, why not make a totally counterintuitive move and give yourself room to fail? God gives us this kind of room all the time. This will help put your heart in sync with God's and can make you more gracious, forgiving, and patient (with yourself and others).

SLOTH

"A slothful person," Robert McCracken wrote, is a person who "believes in nothing, cares for nothing, seeks to know nothing, interferes with nothing, enjoys nothing, loves nothing, hates nothing, finds purpose in nothing, lives for nothing, and only remains alive because there is nothing he would die for."[16] Sloth is "a sad, restless, and ungrateful boredom in the face of spiritual good. It is spiritual joylessness, carelessness, jadedness, thanklessness, unfruitfulness, lovelessness, and hopelessness."[17]

The sin of sloth defers what should be done right away and often replaces it with an activity that is less important but more palatable. This is how sloth covers its tracks. Instead of doing the hard thing and approaching that coworker about that issue, you work around the clock on another project, convinced that it takes priority. Instead of finding a healthy work-and-life balance so that you can be with your family, you tell yourself that people just don't understand what your job is like, and you work all the harder. Instead of working out what it means to be a person of faith on the job, you procrastinate (sloth's favorite avoidance mechanism) and feed yourself the excuse that you will figure *the spiritual thing* out later.

The only problem is that some things can't wait until later. Office politics explode, your spouse may eventually say, "Enough," or for all you know, you may die tomorrow (after working so hard, saving so much, and building all those new barns; see Luke 12:13-21)!

LUST

You know lust is a problem in the workplace when there's a Wikipedia page outlining a "list of *federal* political sex scandals in the United States."[18] It's a long list, and of course it is always growing. Former congressman Anthony Weiner was caught up in a sexting scandal. Former governor Eliot Spitzer hired prostitutes even as he prosecuted prostitution cases. John Edwards, Mark Foley, Bill Clinton, Newt Gingrich, Helen Chenoweth-Hage, Edward Kennedy, John F. Kennedy, Grover Cleveland, Andrew Jackson, Thomas Jefferson, and so on: lust and power playing out hand in hand.

Of course, sexual power has been abused in some workplaces. It begins when you first become aware of that other person—something they said, did, or wore catches your attention. And then, instead of moving on, you linger. A thought runs through your head, and you let yourself go with it. Your imagination begins to run wild, and soon a fully formed fantasy has unfolded. You can actually feel the delight by just thinking it. You look again. You don't really know the person, but that doesn't seem to matter. This feels too good to stop. So then you make contact—a look, a smile, a joke, or a text—and it is reciprocated. Ecstasy! Fear. Guilt. But you keep on going, because you haven't felt this way in years. You deserve the attention, the connection, the intimacy, them. One scholar calls lust

> the intense desire for sexual pleasure uncoordinated with and unsubmissive to the whole person. Unlike true love, lust has no commitment, it is fleeting, and it never satisfies. You are in the grip of lust when you say to another, even if only in your heart, "My needs are more important than your person; you are a means to the end of my satisfaction."[19]

Lust dehumanizes people—both the person *being lusted after* and the person *doing the lusting*. When you give your heart, passion, or desire to the wrong person, in an inappropriate way, you dis-integrate. Even as you are breaking them down for your own perceived needs, you are breaking yourself down. You are turning yourself into a person who does not love in the way God loves. God loves the whole person. God sees every facet of everyone: their dreams, families, childhoods, character traits, passions, hopes, fears, and futures. He knows them inside and out because he made them, cares for them, and has called them.

God feels all of that toward you. He longs for your love to be undivided, so that you can love him wholeheartedly and love those he's given you in the same way. Indiscriminate lusting divides your love and undermines your entire being. "To split the truly important longings and loyalties," Plantinga writes, "is to crack one's own foundations and to invite the crumbling and, finally, the disintegration of life itself. A divided house cannot stand."[20] Or stated positively: "When I respect the image of God in others, I protect the image of God in me."[21]

Yet we rarely do this. We are so into ourselves that we break others down and use them all the time. Companies know that lust and the ill-founded office romances that can inevitably result are not good for business. Eventually things fall apart, and corporate community suffers. If you think employers should be concerned, consider how God must feel every time his community is torn by our lustful tendencies. How are we ever going to experience the Spirit's subtle whispers, God's glances, and Christ's small gestures on the job if all of our attention and imagination is wrongly fixed on another?

Imagine if you treated everyone you worked with as a whole person—not just as a body or a brain or a personality or a sense of humor or even a great listener. Not just as a boss or coworker or a customer who can help you get what *you* want—not as someone who signs the checks, a detail-oriented person who covers for your administrative shortfalls, or the one who takes the lead so you don't have to. Imagine seeing the people you work with as more than just what they bring to you. What if you flipped it around and acted as though you were there for them?

This Godlike selflessness would help keep you from objectifying others.

This is how God views you. He made the whole of you. You belong to him, body and soul. And in the context of lust, it is important to acknowledge that he created you as a sexual being with desires and passions. God made you for the experience of ecstasy: to be totally absorbed by, recklessly abandoned to, and completely lost in a rapturous moment of union—with him.

You are meant to have your attention caught by an *Other*; meant to feel that jolt of excitement when you first see him; meant to be enamored and drawn in, to look again and again, and "to gaze on the beauty of the LORD" (Psalm 27:4). We are made for a deep and passionate intimacy with God, which we can experience, in part, through our work.

ENVY

Envy is an ugly sin that is alive and well in most workplaces. The *Oxford English Dictionary* defines it as a "feeling of mortification and ill-will occasioned by the contemplation of superior advantages possessed by another."[22]

Envy hates that a coworker has what it does not. Here is an unnerving description of how it works:

> You see something, want it, feel that it is only
> sensible and right that it belong to you and not
> the person who has it. Once the injustice of the
> other person having it is established—this doesn't
> usually take too long—his unworthiness must
> be emphasized, at least in your own mind. Your
> own greater worthiness goes without saying. His
> loathsomeness doesn't; it may be said over and
> over, to yourself. Whatever the object of inordinate
> desire—an item of art or luxury, the friendship or
> love of another person, the prestige that goes with a

position or place or prize in life—the world begins
to seem out of joint, so long as he has it and you do
not. The quality of your feeling in connection with
it becomes obsessional. You find yourself thinking
about it more than you know you ought, find it
difficult to think of other things. . . .

Balance and perspective on the object of one's
envy are soon enough lost. If you are clever and
retain some self-control, you will know not to speak
about anything to do with the subject. If you are
less clever and out of control, you will speak too
often about it, thus tipping your mitt about your
(somewhat) deranged feeling. But either way, roiling
within, or exposed without, envy doesn't tend to
remind you of the dignity of humankind, let alone
of your own dignity. If envy leads you to any fresh
self-knowledge, your opinion of yourself is likely to
suffer because of it.[23]

They say that envy is worst among peers. *Why should she
get what she has? She is no better than I. I deserve it just as
much.* Sometimes these sentiments are true. Some people *do*
seemingly get all the gifts, talents, or breaks. They end up
with the best jobs, the most pay, and the greatest prestige.
Sometimes the world doesn't seem fair. The "haves" are born
into opportunity and the "have nots" into adversity. Does
God love some people more than others? If you held the
view that "more" is always better, you would have to answer
yes. But God values us on a different scale. He looks at
the heart of an individual, not his or her stature—physical

or otherwise. If you were to examine God's track record regarding those he values, you would find a lot of very ordinary people, sometimes even weak people. This fact can undercut envy's grip. If you value what God values, then there is a much better chance that you'll be content with what you have.

I think that deep down, we don't want *anybody* to be better than us—our coworker, our boss, or even God. Envy (along with the other deadly sins) must have been insidiously at work when Adam and Eve took that first bite in the Garden of Eden: "You will be like God" (Genesis 3:5). "Why shouldn't we be like God? Knowing good from evil . . . knowing it all?" Only we are *not God* and never will be. God's thoughts will always be beyond our grasp and his wisdom unmatched. The rebel in us hates the thought of this and wants what God has for itself. This is what ultimately needs to be put to death in us. We need to let go of this part of us that never wants to let go. We need to submit to a God who made the world the way he did and, in his wisdom, is letting it play out the way it is, in every single part of our lives. The part of us that wants to be God needs to be put to death.

Envy's defeat will ultimately require something this drastic. The same goes for pride—our overinflated selves need to be completely deflated. Anger's rage needs to be extinguished. The worldview that honors greed's overpossessing and gluttony's overconsuming needs to be toppled. Lust's *all about you* lie and sloth's *I will do it later* neglect need to breathe their last breath.

The truth is we cannot remedy any of these things on

our own. All of our efforts will never be enough. We need to be saved.

START WITH AN ACCOUNTING

God's saving often begins with an accounting.

In order for meaningful change to occur, we need to know where things stand. We need someone with the right set of skills to open our books and tell us how things really are.

In the world of finance, that person is often an accountant.

Accountants are masters of fine print, experts on the smallest tax code detail. They quantify fiscal reality and keep us honest in the face of temptation. Accountants provide perspective and guide us through difficult economic circumstances. They keep our financial lives balanced, afloat, and on course. They bring order to multinational corporations. They steady countries, provide expertise to small businesses, and help grow and sustain our personal nest eggs. In all these ways, accountants image a world-tending God. Even as the cosmos would fall apart were it not for the holding presence of God's Spirit,[24] so, too, would our financial world collapse without accountants.

If you unpack an accountant's passion, you will encounter some of God's passion. If you unpack the accountant-like part of any job—a retail manager closing out the till at night, a warehouse supervisor taking stock, or a contractor ordering building materials—you will discover something very Godlike in what they do.

New Jersey CPA Ralph Fylstra described to me one gratifying facet of his job as an auditor:

My specialty is auditing not-for-profit entities. . . .
Auditing [exists because of humanity's] total
depravity. Society does not trust people to honestly
report financial information.

   People who know they are going to be audited
tend to be more honest. As an accountant, I am
acting as an agent of truth—truth in financial
reporting. In this case, the auditor is exposing "the
light" (God) to what is seen as "darkness" (Sin).
Although I am looking for fraud in auditing and
[for] financial dishonesty, all my clients expect me
to present their organizations correctly and honestly.
They *want* their financials to be correct and true.
They strive for truth.

An auditor is passionate about uncovering what is wrong and
getting to the truth. We want them to do this in regard to
others so that we can know whom to trust. As Ralph noted,
when we are most truly human, we want our *own* financials
to be correct and true as well. Deep down, human beings
want to know what the bottom line is. We want errors to be
exposed and dealt with and for everything to be reconciled
in the end. There is something about knowing that someone
is going to go over the books one day that compels us to live
with greater integrity and honesty.

   In the Bible, Job asked, "Does he not see my ways and
count my every step? If I have walked with falsehood or my
foot has hurried after deceit—let God weigh me in honest
scales" (Job 31:4-6).

   Good accountants are honest scales. They flag error,

highlight greed, expose sloth, and weigh each prideful deceit. While I'm sure it is difficult for a client to absorb the discomfort and financial cost of this scrutiny, in the end it is worth it. Most of us want to live in a fair and honest world. We want a God who will uncover and deal with both unintentional oversights and deception and trickery. An auditor's passion to uncover an accounting anomaly images a God who is deeply passionate about exposing error (intentional or not) and restoring *shalom*. And an accountant's book-balancing joy images God's.

God cares about all things being restored: national economies, corporate books, and human hearts. And you don't have to be good with numbers to feel the joy of that restoration. We all image God when we delight in getting to the truth and then make things right.

We are made to delight in balancing the books—restoring the picture and bringing everything back to its proper rhythm. Our yearning to rebalance and our capacity to feel the joy of rebalancing is something God has built into us, even as it is something that the Holy Spirit is actively inspiring in us.

God will do anything and everything to restore this world, to get it back into balance again. Whenever you see something wrong at work and feel the need to fix it, you are seeing and responding in a very God-reconciling way.

LECTIO VOCATIO

Of the seven deadly sins, which is your deadliest vocational sin?

How does it keep you from recognizing God's presence at work?

Do you want to do something about it?

If you do, you need to start with a brutally honest self-inventory. It may take a few weeks. Start by praying about that sin—ask God for help in getting it under control; ask him to highlight those times at work where this sin gets the best of you. Then write. Every time pride causes you to judge, envy tempts you to want, lust makes you leer, sloth distracts, anger explodes, greed grabs, or gluttony consumes you, write it down. For a month, every time it happens, write it down.

Then pray again.

Go back to your list and start to imagine alternate scenarios:

- How could that conversation with that person of the opposite sex have gone differently? What would I not have said?

- What if I had just held my tongue and walked away from that situation? If I had responded more patiently, selflessly, and humbly, how would things be different?

- What if I stopped thinking that way—actually truncated the negative thought process—and said no? What could I think of instead? What kind of thoughts would act like an antidote?

Then pray again, asking for help in making change happen.

GOD IS SAVING ALL THINGS (REDEMPTION)

HOW NAMING GOD'S SAVING PRESENCE IN THE WORLD TRANSFORMS OUR EXPERIENCE OF WORK

This [patient's circumstance] is difficult, but I think I know what to do . . . and it's in [my] DNA to want to fix it. . . . I almost don't have a choice; that lady is sick, I've got to help her!

DR. MARK SCOTT, EMERGENCY ROOM PHYSICIAN

One place where humanity clearly images God's saving passion is in our response to human crises, disasters, and traumas.

In the emergency-response system of the developed world, there is a concept called the *chain of survival*: a series of actions or services that work together to save a person. We have a 911 call system, emergency-response units, firefighters and police, early on-site medical intervention, quick transportation, emergency department workers, and unit doctors and nurses.

FEATURED IN THIS CHAPTER:
- Emergency room physician
- Emergency-response entrepreneur
- Emergency-response helicopter pilot
- Firefighter
- Nurse

Each link in this chain performs a very specific role, but together they form an interdependent system that is able to accomplish infinitely more than any single link ever could.

Throughout this system, a saving heart beats—in first responders, hospital staff, and health-care boards. That heart is God's!

When Dr. Greg Powell was the director of emergency medicine at Calgary's Foothills Medical Centre in Alberta, Canada, he encountered many emergency situations:

> I saw a lot of incoming people who could have been easily saved if time were on our side. [At that point, Alberta had a 50 per cent higher trauma death rate than other Canadian centres.]
>
> A young woman with a perfectly normal pregnancy came in from Eastern Alberta, and she died just before she got through the door because of a stuck placenta. There were the husband and the baby but no mom, and I thought, "This is crazy— we can fix it."[1]

This passion to move quickly to save led Powell to start an emergency-response helicopter service called STARS.

STARS helicopter pilot John Carson is equally impassioned to get there fast. Within minutes of a 911 call, he and the medical team are airborne. Within seven seconds of takeoff, that team is moving at over 140 miles per hour, heading straight toward the trauma scene. In the quickest time humanly possible—flying in some of society's best aeronautic technology to mountainous locations that a traditional ambulance could never reach, sometimes landing in complete darkness while expending significant financial resources—help is on the way.

Dr. Powell's and Captain Carson's hearts remind us of God's heart:

I will lay waste the mountains and hills . . .
I will turn rivers into islands . . .
I will turn the darkness into light before them
    and make the rough places smooth.
These are the things I will do;
    I will not forsake them.
ISAIAH 42:15-16

In your distress you called and I rescued you,
    I answered you out of a thundercloud.
PSALM 81:7

Like a huge eagle hovering in the sky,
    GOD-of-the-Angel-Armies protects Jerusalem.
I'll protect and rescue it.
    Yes, I'll hover and deliver.
ISAIAH 31:5, MSG

I will surely save you out of a distant place.
JEREMIAH 30:10

Perhaps you have been the recipient of this kind of saving effort—lying in a roadside ditch, riding in an ambulance, or being treated in an emergency room ICU. Those who have had this experience often deify their saviors and call them heroes or angels. Could it be that, in your moment of great need, it really was *God* saving you through all of those made-to-save individuals? Was it his face you were seeing behind theirs?

There is no distance too far for God, no expense too great. Nothing can separate us from his everywhere-present and all-saving love: "Surely the arm of the LORD is not too short to save" (Isaiah 59:1). When we see that arm, manifest in a health-care system's willingness and ability to quickly reach out over great distances, we are witnessing the save-them-at-any-cost heart of God.

FIREFIGHTING AND RISK-TAKING

Saving others always involves risk.

Firefighters often do their saving work despite the danger, in the face of fear, and in uncertain circumstances. Firefighters rush to an emergency situation and then run headlong into the calamity: a burning house, an automobile wreck, or some other horribly broken human situation.

They are first on the scene when a teenage driver is lying broken and utterly helpless on the asphalt, crying out for his now-dead friends after a horrible, alcohol-induced crash; when a mother is discovered sitting on her living-room floor, holding her stillborn child because no one in her family could find the strength to cut the cord; or when a child cowers under a bed or is curled up in a closet—powerless—as her room fills with smoke. Firefighters are there right after the heart attack, the construction-site accident, the chemical spill, or the discovery of the body in the river.[2]

Firefighters go there because they are made in the image of an incarnating God—one who enters our shattered situation and comes to us in our weakness: "When we were utterly help-less, Christ came at just the right time" (Romans 5:6, NLT).

God is a God who is with us in our brokenness. Jesus enters the fray; exposes himself to danger, pain, and suffer-ing; fully engages our circumstance; and then saves us.

Sometimes saving others requires exposure to physical or psychological pain. To be willing to enter into another's suffering—an accident victim's, a coworker's, or even a company's—is a very Godlike activity.

We image God when we are willing to pay the price of engaging raw brokenness. Those vulnerable moments pro-vide a unique opportunity for experiencing the presence of God. To know another human being in their most vulnerable state is a very Godlike way of knowing. God sees that person's pain perfectly. He knows what it is like to hold someone's life in his hands and is totally aware of the frailty of our traumatic human circumstances. God is with you and work-ing through you when you save others. He is Peace in the panic and Wisdom in the unknown. He is also there after the emergency has passed—and especially when our saving efforts fall short.

Only God can give first responders the strength to carry their own human limitations and all of their horribly vivid memories. "The downside of this job is that sometimes you carry with you the full sense of the tragedy," said one veteran firefighter, "a depth of knowledge that you really don't want to carry. Do we have the ability to carry all this? Can we, in our own strength, carry the weight of all of the human misery that we see?"

Only God is able to carry all the pain and the mystery of

all of the world's traumas. Only God can lift us out of the pain we sometimes bear in saving others.

Maybe there is a way of knowing and experiencing God in our greatest moments of limitation and weakness. Perhaps suffering while saving the helpless is the only place where we can authentically meet the God who suffered to save us.

RESURRECTION IN THE EMERGENCY ROOM

Emergency rooms also form a critical link in the chain of survival. Here, too, God's passion to quickly enter into a broken human situation is at work, but in the ER the saving goes further. Using the best that modern medicine has to offer, the emergency room is where injuries are more precisely assessed and then treated. The ER is where a person begins to be restored, resuscitated, and (God willing) made new.

When asked what it feels like to be part of that restoration process, emergency physician Dr. Mark Scott told me, "The emotion for me is almost like . . . you know when somebody is actively trying to die in front of you, or their body is shutting down in front of you, you get a sense that there's something that's not right, like the earth itself is imbalanced. And if you can revive that person, there's a restoration of that balance. . . . [When a patient is resuscitated] there's a sense that there was a rift in the world around you and you just helped repair that rift."

In the beginning, God made this world for *shalom*—for peace and health and perfect balance. But a rift occurred— a terrible fall, a fatal break—and everything *fell* and *felt* out of balance. Things were not right. God stood over the "patient" and said, "This is not the way it's supposed to be . . . We need to fix this—*stat*!" And then, like an emergency room team, God responds.

"This patient's circumstance is difficult, but I think I know what to do," said Dr. Scott. "It's in my DNA to want to fix it. . . . I almost don't have a choice; that lady is sick, and I've got to help her!" And then, with all that he has been given—centuries of Western medical progression, years of medical training, and the world's best health-care technology—Dr. Scott is able to understand, look more deeply into that broken human body than ever before, and respond.

Through all of these things, God brings his best to the healing process. God's resuscitating plan has always included making human bodies new. Every time a person in an emergency room is saved from the brink of death or even from death itself, we experience a foretaste of God's final resurrecting plan. Every time one of God's creatures is brought back to life, we can celebrate and remember the death and resurrection of Jesus Christ.

God brings all that he has to the saving process—rushing to get to us; risking it all; and using all of the technology, know-how, drive, and human potential at his disposal to fix the rift. The God who designed and made the human body in all of its bio-complexity and splendor, who loves that person on the gurney with an everlasting love, is the most motivated one in the room when it comes to seeing healing happen.

Once the emergency has passed and the saving intervention has been effected, the recovery period begins. Here is where nurses take on a key leadership role. Here is where patient care becomes more holistic and personal. Nurses want you to feel comfortable and as pain-free as possible. They want your wound to heal fully, and they will be your advocates on the ward. If things get messy, they are the ones who will clean up.

Nurses know the therapeutic power of touch. They bring all of the technology and learning of the health-care system into intimate contact with the whole of the patient, bridging the gap between badly broken and back home. In all that they do, nurses image a God who cares for the *whole* of human life.

But God sees more holistically than any nurse ever could. He sees the patient from an eternal perspective. His healing view has "forever" in mind. He wants to heal *all* of you: your passions, body, thoughts, dreams, aptitudes, emotions, and relational skills.

All restored, all made new, all—for forever!

A SAVING CHAIN

Within each link of the chain of survival—groups of air ambulance workers, firefighters, first responders, emergency room staff, and recovery ward nurses—it is God's heart that is ultimately beating. And it is his providential power that enables them to do more collective good than any individual person or link could accomplish. As all of these people working in all of these ways come together, an even greater saving capacity results; the "whole" being is much greater than the sum of its parts.

Maybe that truth is also something through which a triune God self-reveals.

In his book *Work: The Meaning of Your Life*, Lester DeKoster writes,

> Imagine that everyone quits working, right now!
> What happens? Civilized life quickly melts away.
> Food vanishes from the store shelves, gas pumps dry
> up, streets are no longer patrolled, and fires burn
> themselves out. Communication and transportation
> services end and utilities go dead. Those who survive
> at all are soon huddled around campfires, sleeping in
> tents, and clothed in rags.
>
> The difference between barbarism and culture is,
> simply, work. . . .
>
> Work is the form in which we make ourselves
> useful to others. . . .
>
> That chair you are lounging in? Could you have
> made it for yourself? . . . How do we get, say, the
> wood? Go and fell a tree? But only after first making
> the tools for that, and putting together some kind of
> vehicle to haul the wood, and constructing a mill to do
> the lumber, and roads to drive on from place to place?
> In short, a lifetime or two to make one chair! . . .
>
> We ourselves couldn't make from scratch even
> a fraction of all the goods and services that we call
> our own.[3]

The difference between the effort of one human being helping another and what we can accomplish together through the chain of survival is *God's* work.

Only it is more than just the chain of survival. Without

other workers, where will the carbon fiber that makes up a STARS helicopter's rotor blades come from? And who will source, process, and deliver the fuel that runs the fire engine? And who will do the basic science that provides the foundation for the training that is given to all of those doctors, nurses, and health-care workers? Who will pay the taxes to fund health care? Who will build the roads and make a way to get to the hospital?

God has filled our world with people who image him in countless saving ways! Mysteriously, behind and through all of our efforts, God is doing a greater thing than any of us can see or imagine. The mystery of the synergistic greater good of our collective work speaks powerfully of the mysterious nature and workings of a Holy Spirit who is authoring all truth and image-bearing vocational capacities, holding this world, and keeping chaos and sin at bay. The mystery and complexity of our interdependent service to one another images a communal God and points to (and in some way illumines) Jesus' dependence upon and service to the Father, the Father's dependence upon and service to the Spirit, and the Spirit's dependence upon and service to Jesus. Your saving part is part of a larger synergistic system that reflects and images the triune God!

LECTIO VOCATIO

1. How does this overarching work narrative (that your job is part of a huge system that God has put in place) change your understanding of your job?

2. What does this bigger-scheme-of-things perspective say about who God is?

Not only does every individual facet of your work have the potential to image something of God's character; now *all* of the facets of *all* of our collective good work also reveal something of who he is. The mystery of our world in its synergistic redeeming fullness reflects the mystery of the Father, Son, and Holy Spirit. Imagine doing your part, knowing that you are a part of this!

This is one Canadian nurse's pain-filled account of the parable that is her job:

> Throughout my short time in my nursing career and schooling I have seen people in pain many times. But I have never witnessed the kind of pain and suffering that I have seen in burn patients. One particular patient was burned severely—on over 70 percent of his "TBSA" (total body surface area). He was a young father and husband. On the burn unit we see a lot of burns that could have been avoided— drunken fire-pit accidents, boys trying to make their own fireworks, things like that. But what happened to this man was not his fault; he was innocent, a victim of something that not only changed his life but has brought on a suffering that I could never have imagined.
>
> About a month after the burn occurred, and after eight surgical procedures, he came up to our unit.

He had a breathing tube (because he had suffered severe inhalation burns) and a feeding tube and was basically covered from head to toe in dressings. Every area of his body was either burned and had skin grafts or had been grafted from. He could not get out of bed, he could not sit up, he could not swallow or eat. He could just barely talk. Every day we had to change his dressings (for cleansing and wound healing purposes).

The problem was that the grafts on the back side of his body hadn't taken very well and he was essentially raw from his shoulders to his thighs. He was on more pain meds than one would think possible, and when we did dressings we gave him a lot more to help with the pain.

The first day I was there for the dressing, it took two hours. Two hours of him pleading with us to stop—"It's too much, too much pain!"—praying out loud for the pain to stop, and crying, "Oh my God!"

Four nurses held and cleaned his shaking body as he cried and pleaded. I remember I was holding him in a rolled position with another nurse, while the others worked on his back, and he was looking directly in my eyes as he suffered. All I could offer was trying to communicate the amount of compassion I had for him through my eyes, and just saying, "I know, I am so, so sorry."

This was the first time I had done that dressing. I had heard it was awful to do, but this was truly a traumatic experience for everyone. One of the other nurses and I told the doctors that night that we could not do that again—"It was like torturing him." I went home that night and sat in the shower for forty-five minutes (yes, sat!). I kept replaying his suffering, over and over again. The next day and for the next couple of months, he was consciously sedated for those dressings—thanks to some advocacy from the nurses to push for the conscious sedation.

After about half a week of him being consciously sedated for his dressings, he was doing so much better overall; he just looked better. I went in to see him one night and he smiled at me. I told him how much better he looked, he said, "Everyone keeps saying that." I said, "Well, you weren't smiling at me last Sunday" (the day of the dressing from hell). He smiled at me again and said jokingly, "I did, you just don't remember." Now I'm thinking, *We put this guy through so much pain, and he's joking with me?*

Here I thought he'd surely hate me, associating me with the pain. But he didn't.

As we continued to talk he shared the story of the accident with me. His wife was there for that conversation, and afterward she gave me a hug and kissed me on the cheek. Over the next couple of weeks, whenever his wife would see me, even if I wasn't his nurse that day she would hug and kiss me.

After his last surgery we finally got his pain under control. After my last shift on that ward, I went to say good-bye and wish him well. When I told him and his wife that this would be my last shift, she got up and hugged and kissed me once again. When she sat back down, next to him, she started to tear up and said, "Oh no, I'm going to cry."

She looked at her husband and then looked at me and said, "We are so lucky to have you . . . Whenever you are here, you help his pain go away. His pain is better when you are here." Her husband looked at me and nodded in agreement.

The thought of being present for someone so vulnerable, and suffering on a level that I think only Jesus himself can understand, and making some kind of small difference in their suffering . . . was overwhelming!

This is why I wanted to be a nurse.

GOD WILL MAKE ALL THINGS NEW (NEW EARTH)

EXPERIENCING THE VOCATIONAL *NOW* AS A FORETASTE OF ETERNITY

Our whole life consists in shaping the present in the light of our expectations of the future.

JÜRGEN MOLTMANN, FOREWORD TO *A THEOLOGY OF WORK*

A few years ago, I asked a friend what he thought his asphalt company would look like in heaven. Since then, he has been trying to answer that question as he works in and builds a real company, with flesh-and-blood employees doing here-and-now work in a present-day world.

FEATURED IN THIS CHAPTER:
- Asphalt company executive
- Labor negotiator

My question clearly presupposes a very material view of what heaven will be like. In the book of Revelation, heaven *comes down* to earth and the earth is made new. Heaven is described as a city with real trees, walls, houses, fields, and roads. The prophet Isaiah foresaw it and described it with these words:

> Pay close attention now:
> I'm creating new heavens and a new earth.

All the earlier troubles, chaos, and pain
 are things of the past, to be forgotten.
Look ahead with joy.
 Anticipate what I'm creating . . .
They'll build houses
 and move in.
They'll plant fields
 and eat what they grow.
No more building a house
 that some outsider takes over,
No more planting fields
 that some enemy confiscates,
For my people will be as long-lived as trees,
 my chosen ones will have satisfaction in their work.
They won't work and have nothing come of it . . .
For they themselves are plantings blessed by GOD.

ISAIAH 65:17-23, MSG

We'll build houses, plant fields, eat, and work on that new earth!

Recently my friend gave me a concise, two-page treatise describing his heaven-on-earth company in three words: *creational*, *relational*, and *responsible*.

CREATIONAL

A creational company is one that will always be growing and will never stagnate.

> My dream, if I can fully imagine it, would be to
> build a company that continually renews itself by the

creation of new ideas, processes, and technologies; striving to be better tomorrow than we are today. A company grows through movement—moving from what works today to what is needed [in order] to be better for tomorrow. It is also very important to realize that the world is ever changing around us. A company must move in harmony with what is happening around it.

This dream, from an asphalt company executive, makes perfect sense to me. If heaven on earth is going to be a real place where we do real work for the rest of eternity, then the nature of that work will have to be both ever-renewing and in perfect harmony with all that is happening in that heavenly city. Some might think that the perfection of heaven means that everything will be done—complete. But I wonder whether heaven's perfection will be of a different nature: always growing, always changing, and always *more*. Even as we will need an eternity to engage in the never-ending process of knowing and enjoying God, so too will it take forever to build that heavenly city. The two might even work hand in hand, with an ever-perfecting city acting as an icon through which we will know God more!

Imagine that.

I think business leaders already do. When here-and-now business leaders dream about building a company that is always re-creating itself and always doing things better, they are embodying a passion that will one day find full expression in the life hereafter (whether they believe in heaven or not!). We are made to work in ever-renewing ways. When we experience joy in taking a company, team, class, or crew to the next level, we are giving evidence of the fact that we are *made for* another world—our present-day world, made new. The inherent joy of figuring out the next best thing is a foretaste of what we will one day be doing forever.

Building something new inspires the imagination and helps you dream of what the future could be and imagine what both the world and work would look like when done perfectly. . . . The greatest thrill in business for me is to have a challenge that is unique to us and after some research finding out that there is little or no advice available to give you the answer. Those moments, when we bring everyone together and inspire new thoughts and new ideas and eventually a solution that we are all eager to try . . . when it works—wow, what a feeling!

When I asked my friend whether he had ever connected his here-and-now passion for new ideas, processes, and technologies with his then-and-there eternal work of building an ever-flourishing eternal city, he responded:

I can honestly say that I have never stepped back from anything I have done at work and said to myself that this must be what it is like in heaven. . . . What I do know and what I have felt is a sense of affirmation, even peace, in certain situations— a moment that is beyond a pat on the back for a good job. When that happens, it can only be described as a God-present feeling, as if something is going on that is beyond words and certainly beyond anything I can do apart from him. I'm thinking that those times are a pointer to what an ever-flourishing city would be like. Where everything we do is deeply connected to God's will and desire for us and for creation. In heaven, I imagine we would feel like that all the time. I think [that] to fully understand that today would cause me to tremble and fall flat on my face before him. It would be that powerful . . . if I can imagine it.

RELATIONAL

A relational company is one that is

built on the shoulders of the people who work there. To describe a company operating perfectly in heaven, to me, describes a company that behaves like a well-balanced family: each takes their role of parent, sibling, or child. Roles of support, encouragement, discipline, education, and training each have their place in any given day. I imagine that when we operate best is when we operate as one unit for a common goal. The common goal has to be pure—something everyone can believe in and that everyone has some element of pride in achieving. Continually motivating others toward a common goal will allow each person to grow personally and let their talent shine.

Our capacity to relate is a significant way in which we image a relational God. If heaven is going to be a place where relationships are finally done right—both with God and with one another—then valuing, embodying, and striving for relational wholeness in the workplace today is, again, practicing what we will value, embody, and strive for when heaven meets earth.

In that place, we all will be united in the greatest common goal imaginable—knowing and enjoying God forever. Again, I imagine that perfect relational wholeness may not be a static thing. Even as we will be knowing God more and more, forever, perhaps we will also be knowing one another more and more—just as a marriage, friendship, or mentor/mentee relationship can get better over time. On that new earth we will know God, ourselves, and one another more and more, forevermore!

I expect that *knowing* will also play out in terms of our work. When heaven is finally and fully here on earth, each of our image-bearing, *embodied-parable lives* at work will be perfectly iconic. Others will see God through what we do. And as we spend the rest of eternity becoming more like Christ (a goal we will never attain, of course), others will see more and more and more of him. As I have written elsewhere:

> The thought of what that kind of new world might be like fills me with awe and trembling. I imagine that every communal interaction will come with a sense of translucence. As I experience the love of another—helping me, encouraging me, making me laugh, teaching me—I'll be able to see right through

that person to the God who is help, encouragement, laughter, and wisdom. And as I do the same for others—support them, play games with them, listen to them—I'll have a clear sense of the God of all support, play, and listening doing all of these good actions through me. I'll be co-loving with Christ, co-listening through him—and all of these interactions will be saturated with triune communal love.[1]

Can you see how these two worlds connect—now and then? Relationally respectful and strong workplaces are foretastes of heaven-on-earth workplaces. When you treat a coworker right (be that with encouragement or discipline), you are giving him or her a glimpse of the future, a foretaste of God's heart.

Now turn it around. If, as a person of faith, you believe that you are going to spend the rest of your eternal life on a new and ever-renewing earth, working in perfect relationship with others, then what does that future mean for your work today? What difference does it make? What difference *should* it make?

Recently I read an interesting blog post from the Washington Institute about the nature of Christ's ascension. As Christians, we profess that Jesus ascended into heaven and that he is there right now. But that ascension is not really about a "change in altitude," says the blog writer, discussing a sermon preached by New York City's Redeemer Presbyterian Church pastor Tim Keller.

Jesus isn't simply "going up" as if in a hot-air balloon. He is *ascending*, as a king ascends a throne. In fact, he ascends because he alone *is* the King of

Kings, with dominion over every aspect of reality.
His ascension is his enthronement, "bringing a new
relationship with us and the whole world," says
Keller. As the enthroned King, "Jesus is directing a
cosmic transition plan—one that will bring about
new heavens and a new earth (Isaiah 65:17-25)."[2]

As people of faith, we believe that that plan is playing out
right now. The Kingdom of God is, in part, breaking out now!

Theologian N. T. Wright says that a proper understanding
of the Ascension is crucial for understanding the connection
between heaven and earth:

> Once you start to think of heaven, not as a place
> miles up in the sky, but as *God's dimension of reality*
> *which intersects with ours (but in a strange way that*
> *is to us unpredictable and uncontrollable)*, certainly
> then you realize that for Jesus to go into the heavenly
> dimension, is not for him to go up as a spaceman
> miles up into space somewhere, and not for him to
> be distant or absent now. It is for him to be present,
> but in the mode in which heaven is present to us.
> That is, it's just through an invisible screen, but
> present and real.[3]

It is like the apostle Paul described it: "For now we see
through a mirror, dimly, but then face to face. Now I know
in part, but then shall I know just as I also am known"
(1 Corinthians 13:12, NKJV).

Heaven is present and real to us now!

Jesus Christ, via his Holy Spirit, is at work right here and now, just behind that "invisible screen." Every time we experience a foretaste of heaven on earth—via our passions or our relationality—we have an opportunity to consider where all of this is heading. By bringing the future to mind, we empower the present, and heaven comes down to earth.

So I imagine an asphalt company manager sitting in a meeting with a staff member who is really struggling to keep up; they are just not *getting it* fast enough. There is a part of the manager that wants to go for the quick fix and fire the person, and there is another part of him that steps into his employee's shoes for a moment and feels the exact opposite. As he pauses to do a "gut check" he realizes that, while it is going to cost him some time and money, he should be patient and help this staffer find his or her way. That decision feels right to him. After the staffer leaves his office, the manager goes over his decision. Thinking about his goal of building a heaven-on-earth company, he unpacks that "right" feeling and realizes that it makes sense. If heaven on earth is going to be an ever-renewing, growing, and relationally whole place, then there will always be room for patience and grace. When it comes to our relationship with God, none of us ever really *gets it* fast enough (or completely). This surely won't change in heaven. On the new earth, God will be forever patient as each of us becomes more and more of who he made us to be (plus we won't be struggling with sin anymore). And perhaps this manager will then realize that his "right" feeling was indeed connected to the eternal heart of God, and he will experience God's presence in the goodness of that moment, right there and then, in his office.

Now this, of course, doesn't mean that no one should ever be fired from his or her job. When my friend and I met for coffee recently, he told me about how he had to let someone go for giving company secrets to a competing firm. But while he had to fire this particular employee, he has chosen, out of compassion, not to proceed with further legal recourse, imaging a God who "does not treat us as our sins deserve or repay us according to our iniquities" (Psalm 103:10).

RESPONSIBLE

Heaven on earth will be creation as it is "meant to be"—the puzzle complete and the picture made clear. As my friend in the asphalt business puts it,

> At some point, trying to build something "perfect" is not achievable, is unrealistic, and can be so expensive it makes the project no longer viable. The best decisions we have made in these situations are where we get all the necessary people involved and sweat over the details. Some call it risk mapping, or decision trees, or "if/then" statements. Whatever method works is good. In the end, there is always a moment where, through a lot of thought, one decision seems best. The easy way rarely is the right way. I imagine that, when this process is done correctly, it feels like getting to the point where you complete a puzzle. All the decisions (pieces) are coming together nicely, and the final picture can be seen and it looks how it is meant to be.

In the Bible, the Hebrew prophets called this reality *shalom*. Theologian Cornelius Plantinga described shalom as the "webbing together of God, humans, and all creation in justice, fulfillment, and delight," or as "universal flourishing [and] wholeness."[4] When a business does all of the hard work of bringing people together to talk and listen, and the result of that hard work is a decision that everyone can agree upon, shalom happens (and heaven breaks out on earth).

Part of me thinks that our sense of shalom (and the accompanying sense of the presence of God) will be connected to *how many people* come together for that unified decision. It is one thing for a diverse group of employees within an oil company to come to a common choice. It is quite another when government agencies, environmental groups, and local stakeholders are included in the discussion. But because things are not the way they are supposed to be right now, stakeholders, on all sides, act in ways that are fundamentally self-serving, and true shalom becomes elusive.

It will, of course, be different when heaven and earth come together—with everyone taking their lead from one CEO, with *all* the stakeholders at the meeting, and with all the time in the world, decisions that are right for all people and all of creation will always be made. Eventually that is how things are going to work, so shouldn't we get on with that pattern of responsible decision making now?

AND JUSTICE FOR ALL

A few years ago I was having a discussion about justice with a representative of a Christian social-service organization.

I said something that was probably a bit unfair: "I think you need to broaden your scope of your definition; it is way too small!" I was trying to convince him that serving the needy by providing food and housing, employment programs, and life counseling; defending human rights in the Middle East; or drilling wells in Africa was not all there was to justice. Of course we are called to serve the poor—the Bible is abundantly clear on this point—but we are also supposed to be part of a Kingdom plan where *all things* are made new, where *all* areas of life—law, government, ethics, and our actions— are in conformity to God's will.[5]

When heaven and earth become one, poverty will surely be eradicated, but everything else in the world will also be as it should: engineering, dance, the arts, economics, architecture, sport, science, and education. Pipeline companies, shopping centers, Hollywood, NHL hockey, bachelor-degree programs, residential construction, and financial derivative products will also be made new. And maybe the two—the eradication of poverty and the rest of the world made new— are tied together.

Already we have seen some connections. Because Western consumption has an impact on lives on the other side of the world, we enact fair-trade policies to keep things equitable. How North Americans buy coffee affects South American coffee growers. But what if we are supposed to go further? If all things are meant to fit together perfectly one day, then all things—including every detail of how we work—need to be made new.

Sometimes I think about what it would look like if every worker in our city learned how to discern God's presence in his or her job and then, as a result, experienced the reshaping and renewing of all that they did. A structural engineer transforms her department via a more revelatory use of calculus, which then transforms how her company shapes the kinds of buildings they design. This in turn interacts in new ways with transformed contractors, who are using made-new energy-efficient materials, the latest fair labor practices, and minimally intrusive excavation techniques; these contractors then interact with suppliers whose product-development researchers are doing their investigations from an entirely new revelatory perspective, and on, and on . . . This ends up transforming a city (which interacts with other renewed cities), a country (which interacts with other renewed countries), and eventually the world. Our world is extremely interconnected now, but surely it will be perfectly interconnected then—in more complex ways than anyone could ever understand today.

This change in perspective would be like making the move from giving money toward direct aid to supporting a more long-term and sustainable form of development. Instead of only helping the poor directly, also help them indirectly by helping make the world what it is meant to be.

NOW AND NOT YET

In the Bible, God's heavenly Kingdom is described as something that is both here and not fully here. At times, Jesus would speak about a Kingdom that was so close that it was "within you"; at other times he would refer to something that was still to come.

Right now we live in the middle of that paradox. We

know we are not fully there yet, but we still have a sense that we are close. Often, theologians look at the now/not-yet nature of heaven on earth from a chronological perspective; it is just a matter of time. But there is also N. T. Wright's more mystical take on this reality: that the Kingdom of Heaven is just behind that "invisible screen."

So how do we live (and work) in that paradoxical middle ground? Could a better understanding of how *heaven-now* and *heaven-then* are connected help us experience the presence of God at work more?

In his book *The Heavenly Good of Earthly Work*, Darrell Cosden writes, "Our ordinary work affects and in some ways actually adds to (though does not cause, determine or bring about) the ultimate shape of eternity—the new creation. When we grasp this eternal aspect of work, we will have begun to experience the fullness of God's intended purpose for us and our work."[6] Cosden goes on to found this thesis on the life and work of Jesus Christ, whose resurrected body still bore the scars of his earthly crucifixion (*his* work and, in some way, *our work* done to him). We see in Scripture that his physical body still resembled his "former" self, as did his mind; he still knew all of his disciples and their stories. Jesus, in his post-resurrection being and actions, gives us evidence that some of *what we do now* goes on after death. And while we know that Jesus ascended into heaven after these post-resurrection appearances, there's no definitive reason to think that his body, his scars, his memories, and how his actions shaped him didn't continue on with him. In the book of Revelation, the apostle John described Jesus as the "Lamb who was slain" (13:8).

If this is true, everything changes.

Who you are now and what you do contributes to, shapes, and builds what will one day be. The work you do today matters—both now and forever. God didn't give us this life and these jobs just to throw them all away in the end. They are part of his amazing end product!

Theologian Miroslav Volf wrote, "The significance of secular work depends on the value of creation, and the value of creation depends on its final destiny."[7] Your work matters that much! What you create, serve, manage, teach, save, manufacture, protect, grow, develop, understand, communicate, provide, transport, and discover will in some way, shape, or form be part of that eternal city. When you think about your work in this heaven-on-earth context, a connecting line is drawn between heaven-now and heaven-then.

And this line doesn't just represent a cognitive connection between *then* and *now*, nor is it just a pointer to some future reality. It is also a line that pulls us.[8] Right now, God is calling you from that future perfect place. The one standing behind the invisible screen is whispering and drawing you to himself. Already our lives are orbiting God's new earth and, in a real way, being impacted by its gravitational pull.

Catholic writer John Bentley Mays wrote that

> the Kingdom of God is now among us, threatening
> to explode at any time from the happenings of
> ordinary life with life-giving energy, novelty and
> intensity. This possibility is experienced in everyday
> existence by Christians, contemporary Catholic
> philosopher John D. Caputo has written, as
> "something stirring, something signaling us from

afar, something waiting for us to catch up, something inviting, promising, provoking."[9]

This is a hopeful thought. God *is* going to get us there. God *wants* to get us there. God wants us to know him in all things, and God will, in his time, draw us to himself. And maybe one day we will see the connection; as he continues to pull us closer and closer, we will get a clearer sense of how our lives fit into the end product he is creating. That pulling action may help us let go of all of our over-striving and self-making. Knowing that God is the one responsible for getting us there may free us up to trust more, enjoy the ride more, and see his face more in all we do.

God is taking what you do at work and reshaping and renewing it for use in his future city!

LABOR NEGOTIATING ON EARTH AS IT IS IN HEAVEN

Recently, I read a labor-relations story that looked a lot as if heaven was breaking out on earth. It was creational (in terms of finding a better way to do labor negotiations), relational (in terms of the listening that happened on all sides), and responsible (in that it dealt with the problem)—and the end result was justice (and honor and glory) for all.

In 2009, the Canadian province of New Brunswick was facing a significant pension obligation shortfall. As many jurisdictions in North America experienced, the global financial crash of 2008 had devastated the investments of provincial nurses and health-care employees. The onslaught of baby boomer retirees would soon be drawing benefits as well. One actuary estimated that future benefits would have to be cut by close to 60 percent! None of the stakeholders wanted this, so they hired an outside consultant who brought all of the parties together to see if they could find another way.

They had to make tough decisions—increasing contributions and cutting benefits to both current and retired union members, delaying the retirement age, and increasing taxpayer support. The prescription would be hard to swallow for everyone, and the solubility of the pension plan hung in the balance. This led one union leader to realize that "transparency was essential; we told [the union members] what was happening and they trusted us to do the right thing."[10]

After months of work through both the courts and negotiations, representatives of both the government and unions came up with a solution based on a very successful model that had been implemented in the Netherlands (which has one of the soundest pension systems in the world). Each party was taking a big risk in the concessions they made. Because both sides were willing to sacrifice and because of the honesty, humility, and mutual respect they brought to the table, a long-term, balanced, and sustainable plan was achieved—a shared-risk plan that was fair to all stakeholders (taxpayers and employees).

After announcing the deal to the public, the provincial premier, the consultants, and the union leaders headed to the legislative building to vote the deal into law. This is how *The Globe and Mail* reported on that event:

Expecting to watch the session from the gallery,
the five [union representatives and consultants]

were instead escorted to the carpeted floor of the Assembly Chamber, where they were given seats on a wooden bench facing [Premier] Alward. After the premier gave a speech explaining the significance of the new shared-risk pension plan, which would also be applied that day to MLA [members of the legislative assembly] pensions, Alward asked his guests to stand as he thanked them for their co-operation. As they rose, the two-storey chamber was soon filled with thunderous applause. Every attending MLA from the two elected Liberal and Conservative parties stood to give the unions and the labour lawyer a standing ovation. Stunned by the reaction, [Sue] Rowlands, the hard-nosed labour lawyer, began to cry. "Other than the day I was married it was the happiest day of my life. No one was playing silly buggers with politics. New Brunswick was fixing its pensions."[11]

Stories like this give us a glimpse of what it might be like on God's new earth.

LECTIO VOCATIO

What is the best thing you do at work—that signature move where you make the greatest difference, feel most alive, and image God most clearly?

Now try to imagine doing that activity in perfection, in a new heaven on earth, forever.

- Would what you do in your job be *needed* in a perfect heaven on earth? (Will we need hospitals, police officers, or EMTs?)

- How would you doing your work in perfection create more relational fullness in this heaven on earth? Take what you have imagined about your work being done perfectly and put it alongside coworkers—people you would serve, inspire, or lead. How would everyone become more? How would humanity collectively image God more fully?

- How does knowing that the *good you do now* will be a part of eternity (continuing in some mysterious perfected form) change your day-to-day vocational perspective? How would things change if you considered this kind of future impact?

PART FOUR

HOW CAN WE MORE EFFECTIVELY AND CONSISTENTLY IMAGE GOD THROUGH OUR WORK?

STEPPING INTO THE STORY THAT IS YOUR JOB

DISCERNING YOUR GOD-SPOKEN VOCATIONAL LIFE

We can make our plans, but the LORD determines our steps.

PROVERBS 16:9, NLT

....

One of the most confounding paradoxes of our faith is the belief that God is sovereign and in control *and* that human beings are autonomous and have free will. Like most God-things, this is an inexplicable mystery—one that we need to step into in order to engage the story that is our jobs.

The psalmist wrote:

Unless the LORD builds the house,
    the builders labor in vain.
Unless the LORD watches over the city,
    the guards stand watch in vain.

PSALM 127:1

FEATURED IN THIS CHAPTER:
- Hairstylist
- Father

In a paper on the theology of sleep, Jason McMartin expanded on this psalm:

On the one hand, the psalm affirms that God's action is necessary for the successful completion of the

143

activities to which we put our efforts. At the same time, the psalm assumes that human effort will be engaged in these projects as well; the psalm should not be read as license for lassitude. In particular, verse 1 sets divine activity and human activity in parallel: "unless the Lord builds . . . those who build . . . unless the Lord watches . . . the watchman stays awake." The same conjunction is present in the third verse as well. Only through the congruence of human and divine action do the outcomes come about. This means that we must strike a balance between pure activity and pure passivity with respect to work. The premise of the passage is that God works, and that God's work is that around which human work revolves.[1]

This is similar to how our planet revolves around the sun. Or how a movie involves the congruent work of director, producer, and actor.

In order to step into the story that is your work, you need to become like an actor on a stage, acknowledging that you only play a part in what is playing out.

YOUR SPOKEN LIFE

Have you ever had a moment at work that felt as if it was being spoken, written, or sketched by another?

It may last for only a second, but when it happens, you have this sense that circumstances are playing out on purpose, that they are heading somewhere, and that there is a plot. Even though you know you are the one making choices, it is as though you are living into a script that in some mysterious way has already been written. The beauty, clarity, creativity, or goodness of what you are doing seems a bit *too* good, *too* wonderful, *too* outside-of-yourself to be solely sourced in you. It is as if you are part of a story that God is authoring and speaking in real time.

There is a spokenness to all of life, of course, but one important place where it happens is at work.

This can happen to me when I'm preaching—having a sense that my words aren't mine, even though I'm speaking them. They are more eloquent than I'm capable of and carry a poignancy, power, and efficacy that are beyond me. When these moments happen, it feels as if everyone in the congregation also *knows* that something bigger is going on, that someone else is speaking.

You would expect (or at least hope for) that to happen in a church through the work of a preacher, but if God truly is speaking the embodied parable that is you doing your job, then shouldn't you have these kinds of moments as well? After all, your work is every bit as much a ministry!

Following are a few ways to more fully identify and enter into the *spokenness* of your job.

RECEIVING

One of the best ways to learn how to identify the spokenness of your job is to listen to what God might be saying through *another* person's work. Ideally, this would be someone whose work has had a direct and beneficial impact on you: a nurse who helped you in the waiting room, a retailer who helped you find what you were looking for, or a mentor who gave you some wise new perspective. There are several reasons why this is a good starting point.

First, it is easier to discern God's voice through *someone else's* job (it is hard to observe yourself objectively). By honing your ability to read God's word in another person's work, you grow your capacity to read his word in your own.

Second, by applying this discernment process to work that directly *benefits* you, you increase the odds of encountering God's activity there. By definition, God is always working for your best interest.

Third, when someone's work benefits you, you become *more yourself.* When you are more yourself, you are more of who God made you to be, and you have more of yourself with which to discern God's work in your life.

And fourth, there is something very important about the stance of *receiving* that aids in discerning the spokenness of life. All of life is a gift from God. Everything is received. To be in a receptive stance—needing, open, vulnerable, and trusting—is to acknowledge the basic state of your reality. There is something about the humility of that place that is crucial to discerning the spokenness of one's life and work.

For years I have sat in the same hairstylist's chair, trying to discern what God was saying through her job. Talk about a trusting and vulnerable place! Every month or so, I put a part of my identity into her hands. And as the grateful recipient of the good graces of her hairstyling expertise, I was aesthetically made new and became a little bit more myself again. Receiving the goodness of her work, I came to understand a little bit more of God's identity-renewing nature.

Think about it. A stylist holds your head as you lean back into a washing basin. With her own hands she washes your hair and, if you are lucky, gives you a scalp massage. After she towel-dries you and moves you to the chair, she then takes a part of who you physically are—your hair—and cuts it, reshapes it, and (for some) recolors it! A stylist touches your body and uses sharp instruments near your eyes, and you sit there, wide open to this very intimate aesthetic intervention.

In order to see God's hand at work in the parable of another person's job, you have to let their good work touch you. God knows every intimate detail of who you are—your flaws, your gray areas, the places where you are thinning— and he wants to make every square inch of your being and body new. He wants to shape you—to wash, cut, dry, and style your life. When you receive the good work of another human being at an intimate level, you become a more trusting and open person. Openness is key to seeing God at work. When you put yourself in the hands of another, you become *more of the kind of person who is comfortable in the hands of Another*. This is the optimal position to be in to see God's hands holding you. Every visit to the salon is an opportunity to grow in your capacity to be aware of and receive God's intimate touch wherever you work.

Discussing what she loved most about her work, my stylist said, "Hearing the words 'I trust you.'" Customers often step into her salon totally exasperated and give her total freedom to cut and style their hair in whatever way she thinks best. Knowing hair the way she does, assessing a person's face shape, and considering their overall look, she will come up with something her customer could never have imagined, often to their great delight. But it takes trust to get there. You need to let go and put your life in another's hands. It is only then that you will be able to experience the delight—both yours and that of the one who is making you over.

Just as a stylist delights in being given this kind of trust, God does too.

God wants you to become fully you. He desires the best for your life and has a maker's heart to know what it will take to get you there. Saying "I trust you" can take many forms in a vocational context. When you extend trust, you make room for God to *prove* himself trustworthy; in a sense you free space for God to intervene in a powerful new way. Even as a stylist relishes a time when she has complete freedom to make someone new—her sense of responsibility growing, her creative adrenaline starting to pump, her desire to do *her best* now piqued—God must surely rise to the occasion as well. This is what happens when you submit your will to his. In that new place of increased *will alignment*, you discover that he is closer to you than you realize.

NAMING

The moments when I have been most aware of my life being part of God's story have been those times when people have recognized and *named it* for me—when they have expressed gratitude for what I do and how I listened, spoke, and acted. It is at those times when I realize that God is saying, doing, and accomplishing something through my life. At times like this I inevitably feel closer to God; his presence is made clear as someone I have served *names his good work in me.*

I have been a part of those naming moments for others on many occasions. I have seen the excitement on an epigenetic researcher's face as I have connected the essence of his field of study to God's truth in the second commandment.[2] I have witnessed the tears in the eyes of a corporate real-estate executive as he sees the profound connection between his passions and God's. I have observed a sense of validation pouring over a server when she came to realize that her serving passion is powerfully Christlike. I have seen in a mirror the trembling loss of words that comes to my stylist every time I name another part of what she does in relation to the making-new heart of God.

Naming is a powerful way to recognize the parable that is your job. As you name where God is at work in others and begin to see the story God is speaking through them, you grow your *vocational parable-reading capacity*. Soon you start to discern universal principles that apply to the spokenness of all jobs. The emergency room doctor's passion to save also applies to your job. The stylist's desire to make things new is a desire that God has put into all of us so that all things can be made new. A judge's God-imaging passion for justice gets planted more deeply into our psyches and we become more Godlike as a result. As this naming and reclaiming of the work of God in others grows, so does our capacity to enter into the spokenness of work.

In the book of Genesis, one of Adam's great privileges was naming the animals that God had made. In the Bible, the process of naming carried a great deal of value and importance. A name expressed "the essential nature of its bearer; to know the name is to know the person."[3] As Adam's descendants, we have the great privilege of discerning and then naming the essence and nature of a particular part of God's good creation. We are called to do this naming for all of creation, including the providentially spoken parabolic nature of our jobs.

Whom do you trust to come alongside and translate for you?

Perhaps it is time that someone named the true God-spoken essence of what you do at work. Imagine that moment when you hear that spoken for the first time and get a sense of the person and presence of God at work—when you actually experience your part in his story!

CO-FEELING, CO-ACTING, AND CO-EVERYTHING

Co-feeling and co-acting are two other ways of entering into the spokenness of your work and life. Instead of relying solely on an outside voice to name God's goodness in what you do or waiting to realize it for yourself in retrospect, co-feeling and co-acting are real-time opportunities to mystically enter into the story of your job.

This idea first came to me as I was sitting in my living room across from my oldest son, staring at him while he did his university studies. As I thought about the young man he had become, my heart swelled with pride. I felt a deep joy and gratitude for his sensitivity, intellect, and goodness. As I was feeling all of this fatherly love for my son, it struck me that God must surely feel this toward him as well! And then I wondered whether God had put the capacity to feel pride for a son in me on purpose. If God was the source of this capacity, then perhaps he was also co-feeling it with me, or perhaps I was co-feeling it with *him*, or maybe the only thing that I was experiencing in that moment was *God's love* for my son flowing through me. Standing back a bit further, I wondered whether the pride I felt for my son was also a pride God felt for *me* as his son.

What I realized in that moment was that every yearning; desire; expression of love; good emotion; and true, just, or meaningful action is filled with the potential for this kind of mystical math: to know that God put the capacity to feel that way in you, to know that he feels the same, to enter into the wonderful paradox of not knowing whose feelings you are feeling (God's or yours), and then to realize that the good thing you feel for another, God feels for you, too!

Imagine integrating this kind of co-feeling or co-acting into all of your life. Every time you forgive your child, you can know the forgiving presence of God. Every time you create, persevere, turn the other check, save someone, serve, build, hypothesize, mediate, or selflessly submit, you can co-feel and co-do it with God.

We see evidence of this synonymous worldview in yet another psalm:

> The king rejoices in your strength, LORD.
> How great is his joy in the victories you give!
>
> You have granted him his heart's desire
> and have not withheld the request of his lips.
> You came to greet him with rich blessings
> and placed a crown of pure gold on his head.

He asked you for life, and you gave it to him—
    length of days, for ever and ever.
Through the victories you gave, his glory is great;
    you have bestowed on him splendor and majesty.
Surely you have granted him unending blessings
    and made him glad with the joy of your presence.
For the king trusts in the LORD;
    through the unfailing love of the Most High
    he will not be shaken.

Your hand will lay hold on all your enemies;
    your right hand will seize your foes.
When you appear for battle,
    you will burn them up as in a blazing furnace.

The LORD will swallow them up in his wrath,
    and his fire will consume them.
You will destroy their descendants from the earth,
    their posterity from mankind.
Though they plot evil against you
    and devise wicked schemes, they cannot succeed.
You will make them turn their backs
    when you aim at them with drawn bow.

Be exalted in your strength, LORD;
    we will sing and praise your might.
PSALM 21

Notice how the psalmist bracketed the thankful content of his poem with a clear focus on God's strength: "The king rejoices in your strength, LORD" (first verse) and "Be exalted in your strength, LORD; we will sing and praise your might" (last verse). And then, between those two verses, he commingled the strength of God with the strength given to the king. At times you can almost confuse the two. Which may be the point.

Success for this particular king is *God's strength manifested in the story God has written through his rule.* Everything the king has, has been granted to him; each gift is emblematic of the Giver, each received with a sense of mystery—with a sense of being no more deserving or undeserving than the next person.

So whose strength was really at work in the circumstance this psalmist was referring to? God's? The king's? Or both? The psalms are filled with these kinds of co-feeling, co-acting, and commingling.

Another story from the book of Genesis also makes this point. When Joseph was being lured by the wife of his boss, Potiphar, he said, "With me in charge . . . my master does not concern himself with anything in the house; everything he owns he has entrusted to my care. No one is greater in this house than I am. My master has withheld nothing from me except you, because you are his wife. How then could I do such a wicked thing and sin against *God?*" (Genesis 39:8-9, emphasis mine). You would expect Joseph's last word to be *Potiphar*, but instead it is *God.* Clearly Joseph is seeing his circumstance from a unique perspective—understanding that his lord, Potiphar, is somehow connected to his Lord God. Joseph understood that those in authority are placed there by God. Perhaps when Potiphar first hired him, he saw God giving him a place; and when his boss treated him well and

Joseph achieved success through his strength and acumen, he said a prayer of thanks to *God.*

So not only can we co-feel and co-act with God; we can also co-follow and co-obey through those God puts in author-ity over us. The apostle Paul states it clearly: "Let everyone be subject to the governing authorities, for there is no authority except that which God has established. The authorities that exist have been established by God" (Romans 13:1). The things you feel, do, and respond to at work are commingled opportunities to know and experience God. Every time you follow the leadership of another, come alongside someone who needs help, share a great idea with another, protect the reputation of a competitor, engineer a more efficient span, choose the perfect color, build something above specifica-tions, teach in a more effective way, lead another person, receive criticism gracefully, or rejoice in the work of your hands, you are in a place where you can have a co-experience with, through, and before God.

IMAGINING OUR WAY INTO THE STORY

One last way to discern the spokenness of your job involves the reappropriation of an imaginative process you often undertake but have probably never considered in the broader context of your life. It seems that whenever you read or watch a story, you undergo the imaginative act of "entering in." You suspend belief as you step into a world written by another. You transition from real life to another kind of life. And then when you are finished, you put the book down or leave the theater and reengage ordinary life again.

This capacity to change worlds is something that we can also use to read the story that is our lives or the parable that is our jobs. If God authors the story you are now living, what would it take for you to "enter into" his book?

We all interact with stories in different ways. Some come alongside the narrator and view the account in an omniscient kind of way. Others vicariously take on the role of the protagonist or perhaps move from character to character. How it happens is complex—something inside us makes a shift, a different part of the brain takes over, our control center shifts into neutral, our other-world neurons start to fire, and our perspective is magically transported into the world of another. And the quality of that world's narrative directly impacts the depth of our engagement. The greater its eloquence, the more kindled our imaginations—and God is a skillful writer!

Imagine coming alongside God as he is writing your life. Perhaps the first thing you would notice is that he is the author, not you. You are entering into *his* story. The ideas, plot, setting, and twists are translating directly from his brilliantly creative mind to the page. As every letter and word appears, you realize that you are actually living them out! It is quite amazing—and humbling—looking over God's shoulder and coming into being with every keystroke. For so much of your life you have lived as though you were the author of your fate. Now you are seeing reality for what it is as you stand there with God.

And then a really amazing thing happens: You discover that you have a say in where this goes! As you begin to pick up on where the plot is headed, you excitedly whisper to him, "What if we take it in this direction at this point?" For a second you are appalled by the fact that you had the gall to tell God what to write. But then he looks at you and says, "Good idea," and writes it in! "I was thinking of going there already," he tells you.

What would it take to come alongside your Author in this way?

The answer to that is as unique as you are. Perhaps there are as many ways to engage the parable of your story as there are people. If God is writing your life in what he deems to be the most relevant and beautiful way, then each of our stories will be different. Some of us will be poems; others might be dramas, mysteries, comedies, or tragedies.

Regardless of what God writes, I think it is safe to say he will write a story that is relevant, one that fits who we are and is deeply resonant. If it is a tragedy, perhaps we will be able to see his mysterious wisdom—just as we can see it in the best books. While an individual character may suffer or fall short, the overall story can still maintain its integrity and be a masterpiece. What if that is the end goal for all things—a perfect story from an eternal perspective?

RESONATING WITH THE PROTAGONIST

Every time you read a book and vicariously become the protagonist, you use an imaginative capacity that can also be used to read the part you are playing in the parable that is your life.

Great authors communicate the beauty and complexity of human nature with great eloquence. Every time they reveal something new about what it means to be human, they potentially name another good facet of *your* image-bearing nature. When we vicariously experience and come alongside that good facet in a book or film's character, we take it into our being. We do this all the time when we enter into a story, in good and bad ways—vicarious glory and vicarious sin. We can use that same capacity to enter into the God story that is *our own* life.

How would that work? What would it be like to vicariously engage what God is speaking through you? Imagine being aware of God's Spirit leading your life in real time as he develops character and generates plot. You may already do this when you look back on your life and see what the hand of God has written.

Think about doing this in real time.

The story God is writing through your life is a good one and is best for you. Surely *this book* is worth all of the imaginative effort and prayerful engagement it takes to get where the author is going. Every time you step into a story—a book, film, or play—there is an opportunity to step back into the story God is telling through you.

LECTIO VOCATIO

Over the past ten years I have been paying more and more attention to the films I watch—not to the *kinds* of movies I choose but more to how they are made.

I have noticed that the vast majority of films that I watch follow a creation-fall-redemption narrative arc. This has given me a new appreciation for all that is good in life, along with both a realistic awareness of the fact that things will break down and fall short and a sure hope that the story will end with some form of redemption.

Every time I watch a movie, I'm reminded of the bigger story God is writing. I reexperience it, I preexperience it, I anticipate it more, and I am awake to the movement of it.

I have also been more keenly aware of those who write and produce the film. There is just something about how Joel and Ethan Coen tell a story! Their camera angles offer new perspective, their unflinching focus on the depravity of the human condition wakes us up, and the way they reveal glory in the most ordinary human being gives me hope.

As I become more aware of these narrative/production details, it is as though the writers and producers are somehow closer to me, in the room, telling me the story live.

I didn't pay attention to these things when I was younger. I just watched the film and walked through most of my life unaware and unreflective. When I was a child, I thought and acted like a child. But when I grew up I put those childish ways behind me—because I wanted to see God face to face (1 Corinthians 13:11-12). And the truth is, the paradox of life being written by both God and us is the precise mystery through which the presence of God can be known.

Take note of the creation-fall-redemption arc in the next movie you watch, and try to get into the heads of the writers, producers, and directors. As you do, look past these story-tellers to the Storyteller, and ask yourself what their ways teach you about his.

EMPLOYING THE GIFT OF GRATITUDE

HOW THANKFULNESS OPENS YOUR EYES TO GOD'S ON-THE-JOB PRESENCE

Do any human beings ever realize life while they live it?—
every, every minute?

EMILY IN THORNTON WILDER'S PLAY *OUR TOWN*

....

Gratitude unwraps the giftedness of life.

A thankful disposition is the only place from which we
fully realize God's vocational presence. John Calvin taught
that in order to "make proper use" of all of the gifts and "benefits streaming down to us . . . [we must] continually praise
Him and give Him thanks."[1]

We can know what our gifts are for
only when we know the Giver. We can
know the Giver only when we acknowledge him as the one who put us here in
this particular time and place. He is the
one who gave us creativity, hand-eye coordination, and a
good work ethic—the one who provided the life circumstances that allowed us to learn, to get into the right school,
or to get accepted into that apprenticeship program and live
the life we are living.

FEATURED IN THIS CHAPTER:
- Child
- Mother
- Scientific researcher
- Man with Down syndrome

Everything you *are* and *do* and *will be* is a gift from God. The more you recognize the truth of this reality, the more you will be able to see and experience God at work.

SEEING THE GIVER

So what does it mean to be more thankful? How would this new disposition change things?

When I was a young boy, my brother and I got a TYCO slot-car racetrack for Christmas. We couldn't believe it! I don't recall seeing my parents' faces as I opened the box because all that mattered at the time was the gift: those red and yellow cars, the matte black track with shiny metal grooves and plastic guardrails, those motorized chassis with real rubber wheels! When I was young, the gift was all I saw.

As I got older, I learned to see beyond the gift—to see the person who bought it. They had taken the time to think about me, what I would like, and whether it would be appropriate; and they gave of themselves—spending their resources for the joy it would bring me. Thinking about this now, I wish I had noticed my parents' faces that Christmas, filled with what must have been a smiling delight.

Forty years later, I called my dad to belatedly thank him for that gift and to relive that memory with him. He could hardly wait until I was finished talking to express his delight. Joy filled his voice. He started to choke up as we spoke. I could feel his fatherly love through the phone. It was so beautiful, after all those years, to properly complete the giving transaction—to say, "Thanks, Dad. I love you. That was the best gift ever!"

Moments after I ended the call, my dad sent a photograph of my brother and me racing those slot cars that Christmas. Staring at the image—two boys caught up in a kind of rapture—I realized that this was how our father saw us . . . this was what *he* remembered . . . this was how *he* felt. And through that recognition, I felt that I somehow knew my dad more, as a giver. I realized that, for him, it really wasn't about the gift. The gift was just an expression of a much bigger love, a love that was meant to be recognized and reciprocated.

In his book *Space for God*, Don Postema writes that a "gesture of gratitude completes the exchange, closes the circle, lets the love flow back to the giver."[2] God gives every gift out of love. God gives you the gift of work as a means of income, as an activity that brings meaning, and as a place to experience his ever-delighting love. David Steindl-Rast suggests that this experience of love, engaged through gestures of gratitude, is meant to grow and spiral upward into ever-increasing levels of intimacy.

The mother bends down to her child in his crib
and hands him a rattle. The baby recognizes the
gift and returns the mother's smile. The mother,
overjoyed with the childish gesture of gratitude, lifts
the child up with a kiss. There is our spiral of joy. Is
not the kiss a greater gift than the toy? Is not the joy
it expresses greater than the joy that set our spiral
in motion?[3]

This is meant to happen in your work, too. That grateful spiral of joy can happen anywhere, at any time. You are standing at a till taking a fast-food order, and you remember that you saw that customer and his son last week. So you smile and say hi and tell them that it is good to see them again. You give them the gift of remembering them. And then they reciprocate and look you in the eye and smile in return. They ask you how your day is going, and a short conversation ensues while you are waiting for the fries. As that customer leaves, you thank them for their business and wish them a good day . . . and for just a second you feel a bit of gratitude for the gift of good human interaction, one of those fun parts of your job. And then God smiles at that beautiful moment as a father would.

That moment could simply be good customer service, but properly understood, it is a moment filled with small gestures of mutual gratitude that enable a growing sense of intimacy.

IMAGINING THE GIFTEDNESS OF YOUR JOB

What would it mean to see all of the gifts given to you each day at work by others? A coworker steps over to your cubicle and helps you figure out how to build a spreadsheet; someone takes your order as they are about to make a coffee run; the new guy holds a truss in place while you nail it down; a delivery truck shows up just in time, and you are able to get the job done; your management plan is finally implemented and actually works; as you are checking your personal bank accounts online, you notice that you have been paid; a client calls and thanks you for putting in the extra time and doing a good job—if you were to tally all of the gifts you receive in a given week at work, the list might be pretty long. Now imagine responding to each of those situations in kind—with a spiral of joy-inducing reciprocal gestures of gratitude. Satisfaction and contentment would result, and you might discover that your job is a lot better than you thought.

What would it be like to be thankful for the gifts at work *within* you and produced *through* you? Thanking God for your gift with numbers, your ability to empathetically read other people, the great report you were able to produce, the idea that led to a more efficient manufacturing process? Consider how your perspective might change if you were more thankful for your innate gifts and what they enable you to produce.

This might feel a bit awkward at first, but because God is the giver of all good gifts, it doesn't have to feel that way. If God is the source of all of the good we bring to our jobs, then we ought to express gratitude for those things. Our inability to do so may be a sign that we are attributing credit for these gifts to the wrong source. Thanking God for what you have to offer really isn't about you at all; it is about him!

Once you humbly take hold of this fact, the door is opened to a beautiful, intimate, and knowing experience of joyful on-the-job gratitude. Because to love and appreciate both who you are and the goodness you produce is, in fact, to image God.

In his book *To Be Near unto God*, Abraham Kuyper wrote about the special love you have for something you have created or produced—be it a story, a painting, a product, or a service. There is something about "giving birth to a thing" that is akin to a mother giving birth to a child, evoking a love that is unlike any other. In Kuyper's words,

The mother is conscious of a part of her own life in that of her child. The two do not stand side by side as Nos. 1 and 2, but the mother-life extends itself in that of her child.

This trait is evident in every product of our own, whether of our thought, of our manual labor, or of our perseverance. . . . There is something in it of our own, something that we put upon it, a something of our very selves, of our talent, of our invention, which makes us feel toward it as we never can feel toward things which are not of our own making. . . .

This trait is in us, because it is in God.[4]

Kuyper goes on to talk about how God feels that way toward you—his creation! "There is something of God in the soul, because He has made it. It bears the Divine stamp. There is something of God's power in it, of his thought and creative genius, as there is in nothing else. We are God's handiworks, no two of which are ever exactly alike."[5]

No one would ever deny that God feels this kind of love toward what he has made. Nor would anyone tell a mother that the special love she has for her child is out of line. So perhaps you are *called* to carry a special love and appreciation, with deep humility, for the good things you create. Imagine a divinely inspired love for the great idea you just came up with—a new way to aggregate data in a meaningful way, a better way to construct that roof detail, a perfectly shaped sentence or phrase, or a means to help that patient find some relief. You would need to put your ego off to the side so that you are able to fully image a God-given love for the idea, plan, product, or service you created.

Experiencing that kind of love for the good you do would change everything. It would enable a clearer kind of seeing, similar to the way a parent's love sees *beyond*, *through*, and *past* any superficial setbacks or shortfalls of his or her children. This kind of seeing would beget the fullest appreciation possible, which would then elicit the greatest sense of gratitude imaginable—gratitude to God for giving you the aptitude, idea, or end product to begin with and then providing the capacity to love what *you* made in a way that is very similar to the way he loves what *he* makes.

Gratitude's spiral of joy could be pretty intense if we got thankful in this way: humbly loving all that God loves—especially the things closest to your heart—and then thanking him from the depths of your being. It would be so beautiful to know your heavenly Father that intimately, to become more like him in this way. It would be so humbling to know that God wants the same for all of the people you work with as well. Everything would change if a gratitude like this took over.

WHAT GRATITUDE LOOKS LIKE FOR A SCIENTIFIC RESEARCHER

Several years ago, I met a researcher at a faith and science conference. This scientist had recently worked at a leading research laboratory and was starting a new company to develop and bring to market a promising discovery.

She was also a person of deep faith. I saw the beauty of her faith when she spoke of her gratitude to God for leading her to this discovery. Like all scientists, she longed to change the world—to improve humanity's lot and to see, understand, and reveal something that has never been seen or understood before. And as she described that moment of discovery, this rational, follow-the-data, empirically driven scientist was in tears and could barely speak. She humbly expressed her gratitude to God for the honor of "being the first human being to see what I saw!" In that moment you could feel that God was near. Through her genuine, heartfelt thankfulness and her willingness to publicly express that heart, we were, in some mystical sense, drawn into the giving presence of God!

God gave this woman the empirical mind of a scientist. He then gave her the opportunity to be educated at the right schools at the right time. He allowed her to excel in her studies, to the point of meriting placement at one of the most prestigious laboratories in the world. And then, in that place, he showed her something. As she followed the data, he whispered, "Look here!"

How amazing that God would reveal this new scientific truth to humanity. How loving he is. What a providentially caring God, to give us the scientific field this woman worked in and then lead her to this discovery.

There is much to be thankful for in that story, as there is in yours if you are willing to notice.

WHAT GRATITUDE LOOKS LIKE FOR THE DISABLED

But what if you are not gifted like a scientific researcher? What if your gifts are limited, broken, or no longer needed?

Do you then bear God's image to a lesser degree? How does gratitude work when you are disabled?

A while ago my son Edward and I dropped into a local YMCA for a Saturday morning swim. Edward is a twenty-four-year-old man with Down syndrome, and the YMCA we were visiting was where he volunteered one day a week. You could tell that he was familiar with the place. As we entered the building he did something that totally surprised me. Instead of heading to the change room after checking in, Edward started running down a hallway in the opposite direction. He bolted through a service door, ran down another long hallway, hung a right, and entered what I discovered was the laundry room. I had to scramble to keep up with him. As I entered the room, Edward was being greeted by several YMCA staff who seemed to know him well. He reached into a dryer for a big pile of towels and proceeded to fold them. I was shocked at his precision and rapid pace! Edward wanted to show me what he could do and where he worked! I'll never forget the look of pride on his face (nor the tears of pride that fell down mine) as he glanced at me in that beautiful vocational moment.

For Edward, folding towels is meaningful work. I believe that God feels the same way. God's heart is for us, no matter what level of ability we've been given. Through the gift of folding towels, Edward is able to attain a level of manual dexterity and high job performance that we could have never imagined (his muscle tone was incredibly low as a child). I know that somewhere in his childlike, nonverbal mind, he's thankful for his work.

And maybe, when he saw my proud face looking at him, he saw something of the face of God.

God doesn't measure the value of our work based on our salary, skills, or performance. God doesn't value *you* based on those things. Knowing this can free you to be more readily thankful.

LECTIO VOCATIO

Here is a thought exercise that will walk you through an experience of vocational gratitude:

1. Think of that "one thing" for which you are most thankful right now at work.

2. Hold it in your mind for a few minutes and consider its source.

3. Recognize how the nature of that thing images the nature of God.

4. Think about where it ultimately came from.

5. Thank God for it.

6. Then be quiet for a few minutes. Wait for a response—a feeling, memory, or thought.

7. If a response comes, keep the spiral going. If you feel God's "you are welcome" presence, tell him why you are thankful and unpack your gratitude a bit more. And keep on listening.

8. In that moment of acknowledged dependence and relational intimacy, remember that you belong to God and that you are made for this kind of thing— to experience the God who gives all good things. Feel the freedom of humbly receiving. Know who you are and where you are going as God looks at you.

9. Be quiet and just be. Sometimes the presence of God can move to a place that is beyond words. Let the joy of gratitude wash over you.

Philosopher Nicholas Wolterstorff once said that "gratitude lies at the foundation of Christian existence. From this, everything flows."[6] Everything is a gift from God—including all that makes up you, your life, and your work—so how can we live in anything but a state of ever-spiraling gratitude?

12

SLOWING DOWN, OPENING YOUR EYES, AND SEEING

HOW TIMES OF REST CAN FUEL AND INFORM YOUR AWARENESS OF GOD AT WORK

Remember the Sabbath day.

EXODUS 20:8

The room is quiet. You're not feeling tired enough to sleep or energetic enough to go out. For the moment there is nowhere else you'd rather go, no one else you'd rather be. You feel at home in your body. You feel at peace in your mind. For no particular reason, you let the palms of your hands come together and close your eyes. Sometimes it is only when you happen to taste a crumb of it that you dimly realize what it is that you're so hungry for you can hardly bear it.

FREDERICK BUECHNER ON SABBATH,
WISHFUL THINKING: A SEEKER'S ABC

My first real job was working for a landscaper named Arie Hasselman. He was a very strong man and an incredibly hard worker. I was a pampered sixteen-year-old who was about to learn why continuing my academic education was a good idea.

Never before or since have I physically

FEATURED IN THIS CHAPTER:
- Landscaper
- Farmer
- Real-estate developer
- Gardener

171

worked as hard as I did that summer. Most days we would start early, meeting at Arie's tree farm at 6:30 a.m. After loading the pickup truck, we would head to the site where he would drop me off with the day's instructions.

One of my most memorable projects was planting a tree in a fairly affluent neighborhood. After we parked, Arie pulled a spade and shovel out of the back of the pickup and walked over to the back corner of the lot to mark out the location for the tree. He took the spade and edged out an eight-foot diameter circle. Then he gave me the shovel and said, "Try to make it about six feet deep." Then he headed back to the truck and on to the next job.

Those words resonated through every part of my aching body for the next five hours! The soil conditions were terrible, the heat was excruciating, and progress was slow. I felt like the guy in a mobster film being forced to dig his own grave. As the morning wore on, I remember worrying that when Arie came back he was going to be very unimpressed with my progress. I was so stressed that I didn't take a break and just kept on digging.

Finally, just after noon, Arie returned carrying a couple of cold drinks. Looking at his hands, I could see that he had been working hard on another site all morning. With little concern he checked out the hole and then invited me to take a lunch break.

Then he did something I will never forget.

After sitting in the shade of a big tree and spending a good half hour relaxing, eating, and chatting, he laid back on the grass and took a ten-minute nap! I was totally taken aback. Glancing between him and my barely excavated hole

I thought, *Why not?* So I lay back and closed my eyes. It was the best break ever.

There is a *freedom to rest* that comes when you are resting with your boss. After all, it is his company, and you are his employee. It is his money, his schedule, and his project. He is the one you are accountable to; he measures your progress and writes the check. So when he tells you to take a break, you take a break. And not surprisingly, because your rest is boss-mandated, you forget about work for a while and really *rest*.

In the fourth commandment, God tells us to take a break and explicitly connects our working and resting to his:

> Remember the Sabbath day by keeping it holy. Six days you shall labor and do all your work, but the seventh day is a sabbath to the LORD your God. On it you shall not do any work, neither you, nor your son or daughter, nor your male or female servant, nor your animals, nor any foreigner residing in your towns. For in six days the LORD made the heavens and the earth, the sea, and all that is in them, but he rested on the seventh day. Therefore the LORD blessed the Sabbath day and made it holy.
>
> EXODUS 20:8-11

Your ultimate boss is telling you to take a Sabbath break. He rested on the seventh day, and he calls us to do the same—right over there, under that tree.

Throughout this book, we have talked about the idea of knowing God's presence at work in more real and tangible ways, as though he were right there with us. This is what God made us for, and it is in great part what work is meant for. Work is a place where we can know our "boss with us," and if God is a God who rests and calls us to rest, then it makes sense that we would have a clearer understanding of Sabbath and know when, why, and how to rest.

But if we never find rest and our work takes over, what does *that* say about our connection to God at work?

LEARNING FROM A FARMER

We live in a time when too many people have no idea where their food comes from. We have lost connection with the source of our sustenance. We are unaware of the crucial role that farmers play in keeping us alive—and how eloquently those farmers image a God who provides all things.

In Psalm 65 the poet described God with these words:

> You visit the earth and water it;
>> you greatly enrich it;
> the river of God is full of water;
>> you provide [the people] with grain,
>> for so you have prepared it.
> You water its furrows abundantly,
>> settling its ridges,
> softening it with showers,
>> and blessing its growth.
> You crown the year with your bounty;
>> your wagon tracks overflow with abundance."

PSALM 65:9-11, ESV

Commenting on this psalm, Duke University's Dr. Norman Wirzba notes, "It is an important teaching of scripture that God is intensely present to creation all the time as the source and sustenance of its ongoing life."[1] Farmers get this truth. They know that they have no control over the length of growing seasons, over soil moisture levels, or over the timing and location of devastating storms. They know that they can't make seeds germinate or bees pollinate. Farmers know that there is a time to wait for God's good gifts of rain and sun. They know that in order for the harvest to come, they need to submit to and trust an entire ecosystem of outside forces. Farmers know that the source of their livelihood ultimately lies in the hands of another.

What farmers know, we all can know.

It makes sense that the deeper we enter into an awareness of God's presence at work, the more we will know him as the providential source of all things. As we experience him through our creativity, rationality, sense of timing, physical skills, or entrepreneurialism, we will be reminded that all of these good gifts—just like the sun and the rain—come from his gracious hand. It is the same with the good cultural products we create though our gifts. God is the source and co-producer of anything good, true, or productive that we achieve. The more we practice God's presence at work, the more we will be aware of this fact. And the more we are aware of this fact, the more we will be able to "let go" and rest.

I think one of the biggest contributing factors in getting our work/life balance wrong is the fact that we believe *we* alone are the sole source of our sustenance. And because we are not as trustworthy or dependable as God, we keep our foot on the gas and work a little harder and longer just to make sure we are covered. But if we really understood that God is the source of it all—that it is his gas, his car, his work, and his life that we are living—then it makes sense that we would slow down more readily and often. Cultivating an increased awareness of God providing it all at work will help us recognize God providing it all in all of life. And when all life is his and held by him, we can more readily leave it in his hands and take time off. God isn't going to stop providing for our lives just because we take a day off once a week.

Sabbath keeping is evidence that we trust God will provide and that we know God *does* provide all things. It is a time for us to step back in faith and celebrate the fact that only he can truly provide. He is the one who is ultimately responsible. So we can relax.

Knowing God as the only one who makes work fruitful (1 Corinthians 3:6) can help us put down some of the control-freak tendencies that keep us from ever taking a break. When we fight God's Sabbath-taking way, we run into trouble and fill our lives with stress, anxiety, workaholic tendencies, and burnout. When we die (in a way) to control, we actually have more space to be ourselves and flourish.

Jesus once said, "Very truly I tell you, unless a kernel of wheat falls to the ground and dies, it remains only a single seed. But if it dies, it produces many seeds" (John 12:24).

LESSONS FROM A REAL-ESTATE DEVELOPER

When I was in my twenties, I worked as a real-estate developer, building shopping centers and office buildings. One of the best parts of my job was doing the deal: seeing an under-utilized, vacant piece of property and imagining something new. I loved the entrepreneurial thrill of creating something out of nothing. I especially remember blue-ribbon days, when a project would reach a milestone. We would run the numbers and they would work, the land purchase would close, the project team would come together, the city would finally approve the rezoning, we would break ground, the steel would go up, we would stand with the mayor and cut the ribbon, and then a few months later we would reach 100 percent occupancy. In those high-achievement days, you had worked hard and long on something for weeks or months, and then it was done!

There is something about the sense of fullness that comes with achievement that makes the opportunity to rest feel more right. In order to accomplish what you did, you worked hard and left it all on the field—and then you took a well-deserved break.

You have felt it before, dropping into a living-room chair after an incredibly productive day. There seems to be a correlation between a job well done and a rest well taken. It is as though our willingness to rest correlates directly with the fullness of our work experience.

The strength of that correlation increases as a person experiences God's presence at work. If there is a sense of fullness in achieving results on your own, imagine how that sense of fullness would ramp up as you experience a day of work alongside your Maker! You would be totally spent, having accomplished more than you ever thought you could and co-experiencing the joy of coming up with that amazing idea, creative plan, persevering strength, or thoughtful solution. And after a day like that, working with God, you would be wiped out in the best way possible. Emotionally tapped. Psychologically drained. Physically done. You would deserve a break, and you would need it!

At times the productivity might not be there—at least in terms of the metrics we tend to prefer and expect—but even then, when we have worked those days alongside God, we will still have a better ability to rest. They might be days where God taught us patience, perseverance, or humility. While we may not naturally see the development of these character traits as a good return on investment, God might. As we know him more on days like these, we might see it that way too. Surely there would be a sense of well-deserved rest that comes after a day where everything fell apart and you learned to trust God and hang on for dear life. And God may see that kind of day as one of our most productive.

ANOTHER LESSON

The unique way we experience God at work also has an impact on the *nature* of our rest. Some of us experience God in creative moments, others physically, and others through their rationality, relationality, or other senses. Even as physical work requires physical rest and mental work requires mental rest, could there be a connection between how we experience God at work and how we experience him at rest?

From a more general perspective, it is important to remember that God doesn't speak only through things that naturally resonate with you. God can speak in all kinds of ways. So engaging his revelation in a less natural way—an opposite, different, or totally other kind of way—may be a very good spiritual practice. Not only will you get the chance to experience something new, but you will also be protected from the ever-present potential of idolatry: "God only speaks to me in this way . . ."

How might your *vocational* way of knowing inform your *at-rest* way of knowing God? If you have a job where the joy of discovery is one of the primary means by which you experience God, what would a Sabbath way of knowing look like? Would it be the opposite of discovering new things—a kind of knowing that just focuses on *what is already*? This kind of break would be an antidote for the discovery junkie that lives in every researcher—a good exercise in letting go.

What would be a way of knowing that is the opposite of the way you know God at work? What new way of knowing him does he want to show you?

REDUCING RESTLESSNESS

Experiencing God at work will also help prepare us for times of Sabbath rest. The more we work alongside God, the more at rest we will be in *doing* our work. Knowing him in all of the ways we have talked about, we will know ourselves better and be more trusting and free. Sabbath will enter into our workplaces, and the line between work and rest will blur.

The more we work with God at work, the less restless we will be in general and the more willing we will be to rest with him.

The experience of work can actually help you reduce

restlessness; you can be at peace as you engage the job God has called you to. It seems counterintuitive, but when both work and rest are held by God and both are places where we can experience him, then reduced restlessness would certainly be the result!

THE GIFT OF SABBATH KNOWING

Of course, more Sabbath time will create more capacity for knowing God at work (and vice versa). Soon a beautiful knowing synergy will result, and we will better know our place in this world. Dr. Wirzba wrote that to "properly be in a place is to be fully present and receptive to its gifts."[2] And to be receptive to the giftedness of life is to know the giver more.

This is what all of life—at work and at rest—is meant for.

God has made us in such a way that we need to know him in our *doing* and in our *non-doing*. Non-doing is crucial for doing work and life well. We need to move beyond seeing rest as being slothful or as wasted time. God rests, and he calls us to do the same. What on the surface might seem to be the most nonproductive time may, in fact, be God's most productive.

Again a lesson from the field:

A gardener discovers that so much of life is unseen, going on in the dark ground even in winter. [One writer] observed that October is really the first spring month because the roots of healthy life are always embedded in the ground and so presuppose good soil preparation. Though vegetation has ceased to grow upward, in autumn, life grows downward. "We say that Nature rests, yet she is working like mad. She has only shut up shop and pulled the shutters down; but behind them she is unpacking new goods, and the shelves are becoming so full that they bend under the load. This is the real spring; what is not done now will not be done in April."[3]

Your experience of rest will change if you adopt a bit more of this perspective. God is unpacking new things and restocking your shelves when you take a break. He is mysteriously restoring you and rooting your life more deeply into his. What he does below the surface, when *nothing is going on*, is crucial for the spring, for your next season of growth. It is foolish to think that a plant would ever choose to skip the month of October.

And equally foolish to think we can.

LECTIO VOCATIO

1. Name your *go-to* way of knowing God at work (e.g., through creativity, discovery, restoration, relationship, naming, unearthing, rebalancing, or connecting).

2. Identify an *opposite way* of knowing from the way you most naturally know God at work. (For example, if you know God most naturally when you fix things, what would not fixing things look like in your times of rest?)

3. Take note of how your "opposite way of knowing God" informs your more natural way of knowing God. (For example, if you are a fast-paced adrenaline junkie at work and meet God in the excitement of it all, how would doing slow, unexciting things balance you out, protect you from idolatry, or provide you with a new way to know God?)

4. Try to identify some of the synergies that would arise between your resting-ways-of-knowing-God and your working-ways-of-knowing-God. How would stopping one activity for the other make things new? How would these opposite disciplines co-illumine one another and lead to new questions and insights? (This happens a lot in our world today—two seemingly different fields of interest come together for a conversation that generates a new perspective that neither could have imagined.)

13

BECOMING A VOCATIONAL MYSTIC

ENGAGING GOD WITH ALL OF YOUR SENSES AND LISTENING PAST YOUR PERCEPTIVE BIASES

The Christian of tomorrow will be a mystic, one who has experienced something, or he will be nothing.

KARL RAHNER

Through naming comes knowing.

EDWARD ABBEY, *DESERT SOLITAIRE*

In her most recent book, *Living with a Wild God: A Nonbeliever's Search for the Truth about Everything*, the prolific writer, scientist, and atheist Barbara Ehrenreich surprised the world when she wrote about a mystical experience she'd had as a teenage girl. She describes the moment as something beyond language; as "ineffable," "transcendent"; as being aflame like a "burning bush."

FEATURED IN THIS CHAPTER:
- Atheist writer
- Investment banker
- Food server

It was a furious encounter with a living substance that was coming at me through all things at once, and one reason for the terrible wordlessness of the experience is that you cannot observe fire really closely without becoming part of it. . . . I stopped at some point in front of a secondhand store, transfixed by the blinding glow of the most mundane objects, teacups and toasters. I could not contain it, this onrush. . . . Nothing could contain it.[1]

Ehrenreich's words recall Moses' flaming encounter in the desert, Isaiah's prophetic glimpse of God, Paul's burst-of-light conversion experience on the road to Damascus, the apostles ablaze at Pentecost, John's illumining vision of Jesus Christ enthroned, and those angelic words, "The whole earth is full of his glory" (Isaiah 6:3).

One can forgive Ehrenreich for calling the "living substance" she had encountered merely "Other" or "Others." Surely she was describing something very much akin to the presence of God. John Calvin once said of a quote from the Roman pagan poet Virgil, "All things are full of joy. . . . Yea, when Virgil meant to praise the power of God, by error he put in a wrong name."[2]

Many of us experience goodness, beauty, awe, wonder, and "just-right" moments of rationality, creativity, and discovery, and we naively fail to credit the True Source. Many believe in the giftedness of all life, that God is the giver of all good things. But not everyone steps into that belief.

In one interview, Ehrenreich drew a line between *believing* in God and *experiencing* God: "If you tell me you want me to believe in your deity, I say, 'No way, I don't do belief!' But if you tell me there is a deity that you can experience if you follow the following set of ritual procedures, I might be more interested. The whole idea of belief is wrong; don't believe—find out, know."[3]

How interesting that an atheist is preaching a gospel of *knowing* God. Doctrinal statements, ecclesiastical traditions— no thanks. But if you are telling me that there is a way to personally experience and know God . . . well, *that* I would be interested in.

Jesus calls us all to this—to know him personally, to experience his presence. That is the kind of faith Jesus was referring to when he said to his disciples, "Blessed are your eyes because they see, and your ears because they hear" (Matthew 13:16). Everyone within earshot of Jesus was physically capable of hearing the parables he spoke, but few evidently really understood what was going on; few *knew* the true nature of the authorship of those words. But the disciples knew. They knew that through Jesus, God was with them and that he was speaking! That same God is with us today, speaking, and sometimes his words, like vocational parables, are meant to be experienced.

But how much do we really know God through vocational experiences? Do we have eyes that see and ears that hear? Are we truly seeing and hearing what Jesus is saying through our lives? The life that Christ calls his followers to is one of intimate experience; we are called to be in him as he is in God the Father (John 14:20; 15:5). We are called to "*know Christ* . . . [and] the power of his resurrection" (Philippians 3:10, emphasis mine). The apostle Paul was adamant on this point. "What is more," he wrote, "I consider everything a loss because of the surpassing worth of *knowing* Christ Jesus my Lord . . ." (Philippians 3:8, emphasis mine).

Paul didn't want to know "about" Jesus—he didn't lay down his life and suffer because of what he "believed." He did it because of whom he knew.

We are meant to know and experience the presence of Christ at work—within us, through us, and all around us. This is our highest vocational calling. And when we live into this priority, all of the rest of what work is meant to be will naturally and authentically follow; we will do our jobs with passion and excellence, be Christlike witnesses, steward our resources well, be ethical, and work hard for the common good.

SELFLESS INVESTMENT BANKERS

I often get glimpses of Christ when I talk with people about their jobs. Sometimes I'm surprised, as with the time I sat down for lunch with a friend who is an investment banker.

Like many, I carried a few stereotypes about investment bankers: they were *all business*, often selfish and sometimes corrupt, greedy, and heartless like Bernie Madoff. *Rolling Stone* likened the industry to a "great vampire squid wrapped around the face of humanity, relentlessly jamming its blood funnel into anything that smells like money."[4]

While I knew that the man I was meeting had a lot of integrity, I did wonder how he managed to maintain it in such a lucrative, hard-driving, and results-based industry. I expected our conversation to focus exclusively on shrewd business practices, deal making, and dollars, but instead I was met with statements such as "I want to help clients more fully be themselves." His words brought Jesus' words to mind: "I have come that they may have life, and have it to the full" (John 10:10).

Jesus came to bring life, to help people flourish and become fully themselves. And in the mind and heart of this investment banker, by aiding multinational corporations with their mergers and acquisitions, he saw himself helping them to create jobs; to better serve their customers, communities, and investors; to pay taxes (thus supporting governments); to develop new technologies; to grow pension funds; and to spin off and support ancillary businesses.

If you step back far enough, it is hard to argue with the results: "Consider what international banks have done through global capital markets to help China and India develop. It is phenomenal: Hundreds of millions of people have been taken out of dollar-a-day poverty. To me that is a social good and in part is the result of financial markets."[5]

The Spirit of Christ must be at work in any industry that enables such economic improvement on such a macro scale. Even though the industry has fallen short many times, it has still done a lot of good . . . if we have eyes to see. And we can thank God for the good that it does.

Talking with my investment banker friend and seeing God at work in the high-finance nature of his industry was a surprise. But what was even more compelling was the heart beating in this man as we spoke. As the managing director of the mergers-and-acquisitions department of a major bank, he kept defining his work as a "service industry." He spent most of our lunch talking about how he loved the *relational* part of his job. Whenever he talked about an overseas client that he got to know better, an office worker he helped out, the beauty of an entire group of people or firms getting a deal done, he would light up. And as I looked at his face in those moments, I could see Christ. It really wasn't about the money for him; he wanted to know and serve others. This banker's God-given gift to humbly bring the deal together via strong relationships was a critical contributor to the flourishing of many lives. To that end, he was a Christlike servant.

In his book *Proper Confidence*, Lesslie Newbigin wrote about a *knowing* that can come only via relationship. This kind of knowing is different from an empirical kind of knowing that assumes that the thing we are dealing with is "inert and must submit to our questioning." The resulting knowledge from this kind of interaction is "our achievement and our possession." Relational knowing is different.

> In this kind of knowing we are not in full control. We may ask questions, but we must also answer the questions put by the other. We can only come to know others in the measure in which they are willing to share. The resulting knowledge is not simply our own achievement; it is also the gift of others. And even in the mutual relations of ordinary human beings, it is never complete. There are always future depths of knowledge that only long friendship and mutual trust can reach, if indeed they can be reached at all.[6]

This investment banker really *knew* the people he worked with. This knowing relationship opened the door to a future depth of knowledge and trust. This may be a reason why he has been so effective in his industry. Through his passion for right relationships, he is very much imaging Christ.

In his letter to the Colossians, the apostle Paul wrote that all things hold together in Jesus Christ. This includes all human relationships. By humbly serving others, Jesus modeled what a fully flourishing human life could look like. When we serve in Christlike ways, *we* flourish. Christ's Spirit gains a greater foothold in our lives when we act in this way. As we become more like him, we will find ourselves in a more intimate and trusting place in relation to God the Father. As Jesus once said, "On that day you will realize that I am in my Father, and you are in me, and I am in you" (John 14:20).

Knowing God at work in those moments of vocational near-perfection, where the world is as it should be and you are flourishing and feeling fully alive, must be something like what Jesus is describing here, where the lines will blur and Christ unites you with God. As Jesus promised, "Because I live, you also will live" (John 14:19). So experiences of God at work must, by nature, have a strong Christ-centeredness. Wherever "all things" are being held together—relationally, creatively, entrepreneurially, restoratively, or in any other way—Christ is present and at work. When an investment banker humbly serves the good of another, Christ is there, too.

And somehow Jesus is the key to it all. He is the embodiment of *God* and *creation* come together—fully God and fully human. He is the model of what the created order (a human being in particular) can be in a fully flourishing, flawless relationship with God. When Jesus worked two thousand years ago, he did so in perfect resonance with the will of his Father in heaven. Because that is true, it follows that right now, he knows and remembers what it is like to do an earthly job in communion with and before the face of God. Therefore, when Jesus' Spirit moves in us at work—opening our eyes and ears to God moments, guiding us through them, teaching us what our work is really all about, showing us how we fit in the big scheme of things, and filling us with a sense of purpose and presence—we can count on the fact that Jesus knows, has been there, and can relate.

Iconic vocational moments are the experiences of a working God through a working Son via an ever-working Holy Spirit.

And very often these experiences come through moments of humble service.

LIKE THE HUMILITY OF A RESTAURANT SERVER

Serving in a restaurant is hard work: Expectations are always high, customers are often difficult, the pace is usually frenetic, the hours are less than ideal, and the pay is sadly minimal.

I must confess that for too many years I was one of those patrons whose expectations seemed to always make a server's job more difficult. A server had to earn my tip, and if mistakes were made, they always knew about it. I was the customer.

But then my daughter started working as a server, and I saw how exhausted she was when she came home. I heard her stories, and whenever I dined out with her, I would notice how she would always treat the server with respect and tip generously. As I got to know a few more servers over the years, I have come to realize that the job they do is very much in line with the serving heart of Christ.

Jesus once asked his disciples, "Who would you rather be: the one who eats the dinner or the one who serves the dinner? You'd rather eat and be served, right? But I've taken my place among you as the one who serves" (Luke 22:27, MSG). Jesus came to our table to serve us. He came to bring something good. He mediated God's providential sustenance and brought God's good graces to us. He took care of us so that we could feast and have life. Jesus came as one who served, and so it follows that *those who serve* are like him. The moment I realized this was the moment dining out changed for me (and started costing me more). Now when I go to a restaurant, I look for the face of Christ behind my server.

As I have come to understand servers better, I have learned a lot about who Jesus is. When I asked one server what she loved most about her job, she said, "The best part . . . is when you can figure out something *extra* to do for someone to make their day better, or more special." Another server said that his number-one goal was to give the customer the best service they had ever had, to anticipate every need before the customer knew they needed it. Both of these servers took great delight in meeting the needs of their customers. More than that, they went above and beyond; they wanted to do all they could to help those they served feel valued and worth the effort. Perhaps Jesus felt this way when he offered his disciples the bread and cup, when he shared stories that fed their souls, and when he knelt to wash their feet. Maybe this is how he feels about serving us now, as he comes alongside us at work. Every good service moment in a restaurant—or anywhere else, for that matter—is an opportunity to recall and experience God's attentive desire and delight for meeting our needs.

Serving others is perhaps the most Godlike and God-honoring way to be a human being—to be like Christ.

Jesus can be known in every good facet of the work we do (all of the ways mentioned in this book and more), but I wonder if moments of humble serving are the most loving and iconic places to see and experience God. Someone drives that bus or cab that is getting you where you need to go. A coworker comes over and gives you a hand with something you are struggling with. A factory worker installs airbags with care and diligence, thinking about the very real people who might be saved by them. An electrician makes safe connections, an engineer designs a beautiful bridge, an emergency room physician stems the bleeding, and a stylist helps you become more fully you. These are all really about service, aren't they? And each occasion is an opportunity to experience our ever-serving God. A lot of common good will results as we serve others, but we don't serve only for that good result—we serve for the person, for restored relationship. And anytime relationships are made more whole, God is present.

GOD THE SERVER

One of the best meals I have ever had was prepared and served by my friend the investment banker. A group of us had gathered at his home for a Christian version of a Passover Seder, and our friend, the chef, outdid himself: seven courses, each with perfect wine pairings. His wife said that he had thought about the meal for months. And we were the beneficiaries! Throughout the evening he toiled away in the adjacent kitchen, ferrying in dish after delightful dish, and when his work was done, he sat down at the end of the table totally exhausted and yet so fully alive.

His eyes were shining and as close to tears as I have ever seen them. A holy sense of gratitude and peace filled the room, and we all were totally sated. Each of us knew that the evening was an unmerited culinary gift from God. Who is able to prepare a meal like this? Who thinks about all of these details, brings all the planning and creativity and an impeccable sense of timing and taste?

Several times throughout the evening, I took note of our chef's delight. And then, as he was sitting there in the chair closest to the kitchen, an exhausted joy filling his face, I looked *through him* and saw the face of God.

We ended our meal with these words:

Have you ever come on anything quite like this
extravagant generosity of God, this deep, deep wisdom?
It's way over our heads. We'll never figure it out.

Is there anyone around who can explain God?
Anyone smart enough to tell him what to do?
Anyone who has done him such a huge favor
    that God has to ask his advice?
Everything comes from him;
Everything happens through him;
Everything ends up in him.
Always glory!
Always praise!
    Yes. Yes. Yes.
ROMANS 11:33-36, MSG

And then, adding doxology to doxology, a friend and fellow guest at the table whispered, "Amen."

LECTIO VOCATIO

1. Recall Calvin's words, "Yea, when Virgil meant to praise the power of God, by error he put in a wrong name," and take note of where you have been putting in the wrong name in your life. Start a list.

2. Recall Barbara Ehrenreich's words, "If you tell me you want me to believe in your deity, I say, 'No way, I don't do belief!' But if you tell me there is a deity that you can experience if you follow the following set of ritual procedures, I might be more interested. The whole idea of belief is wrong; don't believe— find out, know." Make a list of all of the things that you "believe" deeply but do not "know" as well as you should.

3. Recall the best meal that you've ever had. Go back there with your imagination and try to name all of the ways the selfless, serving, and hospitable heart of Jesus was imaged.

TRUSTING THAT GOD WILL USE YOUR WORK

HERE-AND-NOW VOCATIONAL HOPE IN A NOT-YET-THERE WORLD

I know that everything God does will endure forever; nothing can be added to it and nothing taken from it.

ECCLESIASTES 3:14

....

For me, therefore, everything has a double existence.
Both in time and when time shall be no more.

CZESLAW MILOSZ, "BELLS IN WINTER"

....

I renaeus said that with God nothing is empty of meaning. While our experience of work can fall woefully short, it is never beyond God's grasp or totally devoid of God's presence.

These are encouraging words for people who struggle to find significance at work. Even the most unassuming job is not without value. It can't be, if God is there.

FEATURED IN THIS CHAPTER:
- Pulitzer Prize–winning photographer
- Middle manager
- Neuroscientist
- Church builder
- Recording artist

But that doesn't mean we can always *see* what God is doing.

Sometimes our vision is blurred because of our sinful

condition (our eyes, hearts, and minds can't focus as they should). On top of this, creation itself is broken. We live in a world that is bent, corrupt, and not as it should be—one that devalues, underestimates, and ignores the contributions of many workers. These conditions—personal and societal—impact our ability to grasp the meaning of our jobs.

So does the reality of our finiteness.

Human beings are, by nature, limited creatures. We live our lives within the restrictive context of time and space. We are not omnipresent, omnipotent, or omniscient. We can be only in one place at one time and do what we are capable of doing with what we know. Given these immeasurable differences between God and us, it makes sense that much of our work's meaning might lie beyond our comprehension. God may be accomplishing things through you that you have no idea about, that you simply *cannot* have any idea about.

In his book *Wisdom and Wonder*, Abraham Kuyper writes about a sense of coherence that we were meant to know but lost when we fell into sin: "Sin's darkening lies in this, that we lost the gift of grasping the true context, the proper coherence, the systematic integration of all things. Now we view everything only externally, not in its core and essence, each thing individually but not in their mutual connection and in their origin from God."[1] We are so caught up in ourselves that we have lost sight of the bigger picture. Our vision is narrowly limited to the superficial; we have lost depth perception.

In order to see more broadly and deeply again, perhaps we could start by admitting that there might be more to our life stories than meets the eye.

There is a Pulitzer Prize–winning photograph shot by

Frank "Pappy" Noel in 1943. Its image quality, framing, and balance are rather ordinary, and its visual content seems quite commonplace: an impoverished sailor in a small wooden boat, reaching out to the camera with an imploring gaze. When you first look at the image, you have to wonder how in the world this photo ever merited a Pulitzer Prize.

But then you hear the backstory.

Two lifeboats filled with desperate souls meet in the middle of the Indian Ocean. An Indian sailor asks someone in the other boat for fresh water. There is none to give. All the photographer can do is take his photograph.

Moments later a monsoon is upon them. The lifeboats are scattered. Two days later, the photographer—near death—is rescued. The Indian sailor and his companions are lost at sea.

The prize-winning nature of this image becomes clear: This was the last photograph ever taken of these men. None of them knew what was about to blow in or the harrowing plot twist that was about to overtake them. But we do. This larger perspective brings huge meaning and significance to the photograph.

Historian Modris Eksteins once wrote that "individuals and events achieve symbolic power not just because of their own inherent features but because they intersect with broader historical forces."[2]

By definition, God is the broadest historical force imaginable. Christians believe that he providentially holds together and directs everything in the cosmos. The Spirit of God moves world leaders and nations and companies and individuals. He holds all things. And in order for God's great plan in history to play out, *all* that makes up history—from the greatest acts of world leaders to the ordinary fluttering of a butterfly's wing—matters.

It matters because it is part of a greater thing that is totally coherent, integrated, and going somewhere—a greater story that has been authored. And even if you can't see how your work fits in, there is still some comfort in knowing and believing that it does. Your work matters because it is part of God's greater plan. It is significant because he is using it for his mysterious greater good. It has power because his hand of power is aiming it toward his larger purpose.

In his book *The Pleasures and Sorrows of Work*, Alain de Botton noted that we live in a world of ever-increasing specialization. Everyone is doing his or her own thing with no real understanding of what anyone else is doing. This fracturing of reality leaves a lot of workers feeling adrift.[3] Yet this unanchored feeling can also be a pointer to the truth of God's providential presence. Even though you can't see the big picture, someone does.

It is like the feeling you might have when you look at the organizational chart of the company you work for, put your finger on the box representing the department you work in, and think, *There, that's where I am.*

It is like the time when the supervisor or CEO visits your workstation or office and shakes your hand and asks how things are going. Even though you may still feel like a cog in the machinery, you get a greater sense that your contribution matters because you have been in contact with the one who sees the big picture (or at least more of it).

God sees you at work even if no one else does. And that fact alone can remind you that the small thing you do is part of a very big plan. What would it be like to get God's perspective on what you do?

Recently I led a seminar on finding God at work. I met an employee of a large technology company who was interested in my topic and curious about its implications for his job as a middle manager in a huge corporation. Although he had a deep faith and desperately wanted to integrate it more meaningfully at his workplace, he just couldn't find God there.

Later in the seminar, I had planned to lead the group through unpacking someone's job to see whether we could find God's truth in what that person did. I suggested we take a look at the middle manager's job.

As we did that, he described in detail what he did: how he loved resourcing others so that they could fully do *their* jobs; how his role involved taking things from above and translating them to those below and vice versa; how he deeply valued the people he served; and how he listened, encouraged, sought to create community, and struggled with how to hold people accountable.

Each time he described a different facet of his work, I could see how he was a mediator, just as Christ is.

During the group discussion, it became clear that much of what he did at work was similar to what his father did as a pastor—his job was just as much of a ministry. The Kingdom building he was doing at his place of work mattered as much to God as his father's Kingdom building did.

My hope was that this man could "practice Christ's presence" through the mediating work he did. The presence of the Christ who personally knows every employee in that corporation, the Christ who holds the entire company in his hands and uses it as a tool for bringing better technology to his world, the Christ who knows where that technology will lead in the future.

Sometimes we can't fully see how history is framing what we are doing, and often we can't see how our contributions matter within the larger mechanism. And sometimes the meaning of our work might be difficult to see because the meaning hasn't shown up yet.

English professor Susan VanZanten wrote,

> Perhaps one of the hardest lessons to learn [for me] has been to be content with not knowing the impact I make, of living with deferred achievement. A surgeon, an accountant, a carpenter, an event planner—the fruits of such labour are readily apparent. I teach a class, write an essay, or publish a book, and I may not know that it has affected anyone's life significantly and positively for ten or twenty years, if ever.[4]

If ever. We worship an eternal God whose plan is infinite, so for him to wait a few years or decades to manifest the meaning of our work shouldn't be a big surprise. For God, there is a time and a purpose for everything. And sometimes his purpose, or the fullest sense of his purpose, shows up at a later time.

This past year, a young scientist in our congregation published a paper in a leading neuroscientific journal. In her article, she described a stress-regulating mechanism that she had uncovered in the brain's hypothalamus region. It was big news, and as I congratulated her, she was quick to note that what she did was done "standing on the shoulders of giants." The ideas that she worked with were already there. Scientists who had gone before her had already theorized about the presence of the opioids she wrote about. They just hadn't known precisely what those opioids would do.

Some of the scientists who laid the groundwork for this scientist's discovery never saw the definitive evidence proving their theories right. Sure, they might have had a strong sense that they had uncovered something new, and they may have experienced some vocational meaning as a result, but they never got to see the fullness of their work: the day when a future researcher would actually see what they had only been able to theorize about.

There is a fascinating story about how Salisbury Cathedral was built:

> The immense Salisbury Cathedral began, in 1220–1225, as a set of stone posts and beams that established the Lady Chapel at one end of the future cathedral. The builders had a general idea of the cathedral's eventual size, but no more. However the proportions of the beams in the Lady Chapel suggested a larger building's engineering DNA and were articulated in the big nave and two transepts built from 1225 to about 1250. From 1250 to 1280, this DNA then generated the cloister, treasury, and chapter house; in the chapter house the original geometries, meant for a square structure, were now adapted to an octagon, in the treasury to a six-sided vault. How did the builders achieve this astonishing construction? There was no one single architect; the

masons had no blueprints. Rather, the gestures with which the building began evolved in principles and were collectively managed over three generations. Each event in building practice became absorbed in the fabric of instructing and regulating the next generation.[5]

The work God does is of ultimate significance and of the highest order. A project of this scale would certainly take much more than any individual or individual generation could ever bring. It would take all of humanity, over all of time, to complete the glorious work of God. I don't think we have any idea what he has in store for all of us. And if we think that we are already finding the fullest sense of meaning and significance in our work, then perhaps we should think again. For our time and place, what we do may be good, but when weighed on an eternal scale, we realize we haven't seen anything yet! Who knows where God is going with the "gestures" we manifest in our ordinary jobs?

John Donne wrote,

> All mankind is of one author, and is of one volume; when one man dies, one chapter is not torn out of the book, but translated into a better language; and every chapter must be so translated; God employs several translators; some pieces are translated by age, some by sickness, some by war, some by justice; but God's hand is in every translation, and his hand shall bind up all our scattered leaves again for that library where every book shall lie open to one another.[6]

God has a better language that he will one day translate your work into. It is a beautiful hope for anyone who works. And like all hope, it can be appropriated only by faith—a faith that God really is going to make something of this life that you are living, a faith that helps you hold on when you can't quite see God's good purposes through your vocation.

And perhaps the struggles we face at work can also bring us meaning in another way. Sometimes the meaninglessness in what we do can be a stimulus to our *search* for meaning. That broken thing at work—a lack of recognition, significance, or growth—can, via contrast, be a pointer to the God who sees, values, and has plans for us. Perhaps this is another way that God is imperceptibly present in our jobs. The voids, the needs, the brokenness, and the lack of progress all leave us in that place where we have no choice but to recognize that life without God is a losing proposition. This brokenness ensures that we stay humble, real, and waiting.

The Academy Award–winning film *Searching for Sugar Man* tells the powerful story of Detroit-based musician Sixto Rodriguez. Rodriguez had a talent that some in the industry said surpassed Bob Dylan. In the 1970s, he recorded an album that was a monumental flop in the United States. Nobody heard him, nobody listened to him, and he was finally dropped by his record label. While he enjoyed some success in Australia for a couple of years, he ended up living a very simple life, working as a construction laborer, living in a derelict home. He was known for his humility and strong sense of self and not so much for any musical success.

What he didn't know was that his album was a huge hit in South Africa. To the people in that country, he was a household name! His record was one of the biggest at that time, always displayed right alongside those of the Beatles and Simon and Garfunkel.

For years, many South African fans held to the myth that this mystery man, Rodriguez, was dead, perhaps by suicide onstage. But then some music industry workers and a musicologist started researching the story. In 1997, they discovered that Rodriguez was in fact alive. It was like a resurrection! "I was searching for a dead man; one morning I discover a living man," said one of the researchers. After making contact with Rodriguez, they convinced him to come to South Africa for the first time in his life and do a concert.

The documentary footage of that first Cape Town concert is deeply moving. Rodriguez and his family were picked up from the airport in limousines. There was a crush of reporters and photographers. Concert posters were plastered everywhere. Rodriguez's daughter said that the moment felt like "another world." Imagine that kind of recognition.

On the night of the concert, Rodriguez got up to play in a huge stadium filled with screaming fans, young and old. He couldn't start his first song because of all the adulation. For several minutes everyone just cheered! They were honoring him for his work and his gifts and for who he was. He had been dead, but now he was alive again. Rodriguez's first words from the stage? "Thanks for keeping me alive!"

One commentator said the following:

I thought that I would see, you know, him being bewildered at all these people staring up at him. I saw the opposite. I saw absolute tranquility. There

was absolute serenity on his face . . . it's like he had
arrived at . . . that place that he'd tried to find his
whole life. . . . Here's a guy who lived somewhere
else, on the other side of the earth, and it was almost
as if he had found his home.[7]

This is a modern-day vocational parable. Could it be that
your work also is making a difference in a faraway place, a
place you may never see (but that Someone does)?

When Rodriguez returned to Detroit, he went back to
his work as a laborer for a time. His old construction boss
summed him up this way:

What he's demonstrated very clearly is that you
have a choice. He took all that torment, all
that agony, all that confusion and pain, and he
transformed it into something beautiful. He's like
the silkworm . . . you take this raw material and
you transform it. You come out with something
that wasn't there before, something beautiful,
something perhaps transcendent, something
perhaps eternal.[8]

Perhaps God will give you a similar glimpse and let you
see just how significant your contribution is in his larger
plan, in the future, or in another place. Or maybe he will
just let you know that he is there, right there where you
work, holding you, your contributions, the whole of this
planet, and the future in his more-than-capable hands. And
maybe knowing him in that place will be enough.

No eye has seen, no ear has heard,
    and no mind has imagined
what God has prepared
    for those who love him.

1 CORINTHIANS 2:9, NLT

LECTIO VOCATIO

You may need to broaden your perspective when it comes to deciding whether your job has meaning. Here are a few questions to help you do that:

1. If you knew that you wouldn't see the meaning of your work for ten years, what difference could that knowledge make for today? What is the present value of future meaning?

2. If you knew that the impact of your work was playing out in some other place that you could never visit, see, or get reports from, could you be satisfied with that? What would you have to let go of for that to happen?

3. If the only meaning that you ever got from your job was a sense of God being mysteriously, mystically present with you, would that be enough?

THE PARABLE OF A PASTOR

HONORING GOD AS WE HONOR THE WORK OF OTHERS

As a pastor, my deepest desire is to know God more. I want to experience God in his fullness, to know him as the one who made and keeps all things, who reveals himself through the Bible and creation, who speaks through nature and human nature, and whose voice goes out into all the earth.

I want to know Jesus in his fullness—as my personal Savior and as the one *in*, *through*, and *for whom* all things were made.

My greatest vocational joy is bearing witness to God's everywhere presence so that others can do the same.

I love actively listening for God's voice through the image-bearing natures of people at work. I can't get enough of the epiphany moments where, mid-conversation, it's as though Christ in me is listening to Christ in them. When I listen in love, it feels as if *God* is hearing that person.

I get excited when I hear the echo of God's voice in what people say, when their words rhyme with his. As scriptural truths fill my mind, I'm overwhelmed by the synergistic connection: God *then* and God *now*, a timeless God right *here*!

When I *name* that connection, something holy happens. It's as though God is naming his presence at a person's work.

At this point, in the vocational-exegesis conversation, there is always a pause. I love seeing the look in people's eyes when they realize that God really is moving through the work they do. At first they're surprised, and then there is this beautiful sense of goodness and gratitude that washes over them. It's as though they are becoming more of their vocational selves right before my eyes. In that moment I experience God's delight.

It is such an honor to be a part of that process. I get to be God's listening and naming voice. And all of those workers get a glimpse of what God thinks about them and what they do. God cares deeply about them, made them to bear his image in a unique way, and wants them to know him and experience his love, strength, power, and wisdom in all things—including their work.

Some of the most numinous experiences I've had have happened on-site, at people's jobs: naming God's presence in their studio, office boardroom, farm field, or retail store outlet. When I step onto their turf, it feels incarnational. I feel like I'm imaging the God who comes to us. When I'm in these places, conversations feel intimate and close, and God's word through a person's job seems clearer, as though God were within earshot.

A few months ago, I met with a couple of custom car restorers in their backyard garage. Sitting on an old Volkswagen bench seat, beside a half-restored '57 Bug, we talked about how their hearts and passions imaged God's.

As they talked, I made the God connections: naming

God's presence at that moment when they first *saw a wreck that could be made new*; when they *made that hard decision to cut into the body to make it better*; when they *ripped the guts out of the vehicle*; when they *dreamed about how amazing that car or truck could one day be*; when they *poured their life into the renewal process*, using every bit of creative energy they had and letting it pour from their brains to their hands in a turbocharged way; and then when they came up with that new engine, body or component configuration, automotive finish, frame, level of horsepower, way of handling, responsiveness, look, sound, smell, or feel.

Looking back, I wonder whether those two hours we spent talking may have had more impact on the spiritual lives of those two men than all of the Sunday morning sermons they heard me preach.

What's beautiful for me is that now, every time I see a restored car (or talk to my accountant, or meet a nurse, or see a Walmart greeter), I'm reminded of God's everywhere presence.

Having had the privilege of coming alongside scores of people and helping them theologically unpack the parable that is their job, I have witnessed renewed vocational joy again and again—people gaining a clearer and more compelling sense of how faith can be lived out at work, and gaining a clearer and more compelling sense of who Jesus is.

For the gift of that work, I am eternally grateful.

I am made in the image of a God who created work. I honor him when I acknowledge the work of his hands. We all do.

Index of Vocations

What follows is a list of vocations mentioned in this book:

Videos of sermons preached on the following vocations can be found online:

- Police officer: "God's Protective Heart in a Police Officer" (https://www.youtube.com/watch?v=uQ0ofi5UPdg)

- Journalist: "God's News (through a Journalist)" (https://www.youtube.com/watch?v=AhyF4ErTz70)

- City mayor: "The Gospel According to Mayor Naheed Nenshi" (https://www.youtube.com/watch?v=c5yA2ApELKE)

- Optometrist: "Seeing God through an Optometrist" (https://www.youtube.com/watch?v=Tx0fsfQ_5JA)

- Audiologist: "Hearing God through an Audiologist" (https://vimeo.com/121078813)

- Human resources manager: "The God of all Human Resources" (https://vimeo.com/114598579)

- Development worker: "God's Coming-Along-Side Heart in a Development Worker" (https://vimeo.com/78596375)

- University professor: "Finding God in a Professor" (https://vimeo.com/146706532)

- Software engineer: "God's Truth in a Software Engineer" (https://www.youtube.com/watch?v=99mM84FWeWE)

- Artist: "The Group of Seven—Iconic Artists" (https://www.youtube.com/watch?v=yxfkIYL1wnI)

- Midwife: "God's Birthing Truth in a Midwife" (https://vimeo.com/56331987)

- Custom car restorer: "God's (Auto) Restoring Heart" (https://www.youtube.com/watch?v=pIuwmP16eGQ)

- Radiation physicist: "God, Cancer, and Radiation Therapy" (https://www.youtube.com/watch?v=FSU9MPhNkXs)

- Professional skier and base jumper: "The Parable of Shane McConkey" (https://www.youtube.com/watch?v=Ul36H-w5-9U)

- Olympic breaststroker: "The Parable of Olympic Swimmer Tera Van Beilen" (https://www.youtube.com/watch?v=1sxjEKSpCOI)

- Teacher: "The Parable of a Teacher" (https://www.youtube.com/watch?v=jvF_uGEz4Bk)

Acknowledgments

This book would not exist were it not for the work of many others.

Workers who helped unpack the parable that is their job—electricians, mechanics, psychologists, artists, landlords, doctors, researchers, cleaners, judges, geologists, geophysicists, accountants, emergency-response workers, firefighters, police officers, asphalt company managers, hairstylists, parents, molecular geneticists, the disabled, the unemployed, landscapers, farmers, real-estate developers, gardeners, writers, investment bankers, food servers, chefs, photographers, middle managers, musicians, automotive restorers, journalists, politicians, optometrists, audiologists, HR managers, development workers, professors, engineers, midwives, radiation physicists, athletes, teachers, Walmart greeters, and many more.

Thinkers such as Neal Plantinga, Richard Mouw, C. S. Lewis, Herman Bavinck, and Abraham Kuyper, who set a solid theological foundation upon which to engage the idea of vocational revelation.

The Christian Reformed Church of North America for starting new churches and giving them the latitude to dream big theological dreams.

The John Templeton Foundation for funding a Scientists in

Congregations (SinC) grant to explore preaching at the intersection of faith and science.

Publisher Don Pape at NavPress for taking on the book, and editor David Zimmerman for helping it find its form.

A local church whose leaders, staff, and community members freely make room for their pastor to write a book.

An editor wife who loves good grammar as much as she loves the idea of God speaking everywhere.

An artist daughter who inspires my aesthetic sensibilities.

A physician son who teaches me the language of science.

And a son with Down syndrome who grounds me in love.

Notes

INTRODUCTION: FINDING GOD AT WORK

1. These last two questions are those that my coworker Pastor Rich Braaksma asks. He's always a bit cynical when it comes to those who claim to "know how God works."
2. Another observation from Pastor Rich: We don't often apply to the concrete details of our lives what we believe in the abstract.
3. "New 9/11 Video: NASA Releases Aerial View," YouTube video, 1:00, posted by Buzz60, September 7, 2011, https://www.youtube.com/watch?v=0dvTc8pmOzY.
4. "Overview," Vimeo video, 19:02, posted by Planetary Collective, December 6, 2012, https://vimeo.com/55073825.
5. Saint Augustine of Hippo, *The City of God* (Peabody, MA: Hendrickson, 2009), 624.
6. I owe much of my understanding of the nature of an apprentice to sociologist Richard Sennett via his book *The Craftsman* (New Haven, CT: Yale University Press, 2008).
7. This portion on the common good is adapted from an article I wrote for *ThinkChristian*: "Why Working for the Common Good Isn't Enough," *ThinkChristian*, April 18, 2013, https://thinkchristian.reframemedia.com /why-working-for-the-common-good-isnt-enough.

CHAPTER 1: ALL WORK MATTERS

1. Richard J. Mouw, *Abraham Kuyper: A Short and Personal Introduction* (Grand Rapids, MI: Eerdmans, 2011), 92.
2. See Jill Haak Adels, *The Wisdom of the Saints* (New York: Oxford University Press, 1987), 11.
3. Kathleen Norris, *Acedia & Me: A Marriage, Monks, and a Writer's Life* (New York: Riverhead, 2008), 190.
4. Cornelius Plantinga Jr., *Engaging God's World: A Christian Vision of Faith, Learning, and Living* (Grand Rapids, MI: Eerdmans, 2002), 22.
5. My coworkers Heather Cowie and Kayleigh Suggett helped me better understand this perspective.
6. Abraham Kuyper, *Wisdom and Wonder: Common Grace in Science and Art*, trans. Nelson D. Kloosterman (Grand Rapids, MI: Christian's Library Press, 2011), 151.
7. Sam Kolias, interview by Gordon Pitts, "Boardwalk's Sam Kolias: The Friendliest Landlord," *Globe and Mail*, November 16, 2009, http://www.theglobeandmail .com/report-on-business/careers/boardwalks-sam-kolias-the-friendliest-landlord /article4292677/.

CHAPTER 2: IMAGING GOD WITH YOUR WHOLE BEING

1. Herman Bavinck, *Reformed Dogmatics: God and Creation*, vol. 2, ed. John Bolt (Grand Rapids, MI: Baker Academic, 2004), 530.
2. Albert M. Wolters, *Creation Regained: Biblical Basics for a Reformational Worldview* (Grand Rapids, MI: Eerdmans, 2005), 41–42.
3. Timothy Keller, *Every Good Endeavor: Connecting Your Work to God's Work* (New York: Penguin, 2014), 47.

4. "Holy Spirit," in *Eerdmans Bible Dictionary,* edited by Allen C. Myers (Grand Rapids, MI: Eerdmans, 1996), 497.
5. Doug Stowe, *Wisdom of the Hands* (blog), October 16, 2006, http://wisdomofhands.blogspot.com/2006/10/getting-real.html.
6. Cornelius Plantinga Jr., *Engaging God's World: A Christian Vision of Faith, Learning, and Living* (Grand Rapids, MI: Eerdmans, 2002), 121.
7. I owe much of my understanding of tacit knowledge to sociologist Richard Sennett via his book *The Craftsman* (New Haven, CT: Yale University Press, 2009).
8. Kuyper, *Wisdom and Wonder,* 39–40. See also Hebrews 1:2: "But in these last days he has spoken to us by his Son, whom he appointed heir of all things, and through whom also he made the universe."
9. Andy Hoffman, "Alberta Native Stands at Crux of Dialogue between China and the West," *The Globe and Mail,* August 27, 2011, http://www.theglobeandmail.com/news/world/alberta-native-stands-at-crux-of-dialogue-between-china-and-the-west/article592202/?page=all.
10. Ibid.
11. Ibid.

CHAPTER 3: LEANING INTO GOD'S SIGNATURE MOVES
1. Esther L. Meek, "Reading the Bible . . . and Longing to Know," *Comment,* June 1, 2006, https://www.cardus.ca/comment/article/315/reading-the-bible-and-longing-to-know/.
2. I originally shared this story in my book *The Day Metallica Came to Church: Searching for the Everywhere God in Everything* (Grand Rapids, MI: Square Inch, 2010), 151.
3. Kuyper, *Wisdom and Wonder,* 39–40.
4. Louis Berkhof, *Systematic Theology* (Grand Rapids, MI: Eerdmans, 1996), 426.
5. Kuyper, *Wisdom and Wonder,* 41.
6. C. S. Lewis, as quoted in Wayne Martindale and Jerry Root, eds., *The Quotable Lewis* (Carol Stream, IL: Tyndale, 2012), 611.
7. Meek, "Reading the Bible and Longing to Know."
8. John Calvin wrote, "For as the aged, or those whose sight is defective, when any book, however fair, is set before them, though they perceive that there is something written are scarcely able to make out two consecutive words, but, when aided by glasses, begin to read distinctly, so Scripture, gathering together the impressions of Deity, which, till then, lay confused in our minds, dissipates the darkness, and shows us the true God clearly." See John Calvin, *Institutes of the Christian Religion,* volume 1, trans. Henry Beveridge (Peabody, MA: Hendrickson, 2009), 64.
9. Calvin, *Institutes of Christian Religion* I.xiii.18. Italics added.

CHAPTER 4: NOTICING GOD'S UNNOTICED PRESENCE
1. Most of what I know about sanitation workers I learned from Robin Nagle's book *Picking Up: On the Streets and Behind the Trucks with the Sanitation Workers of New York City* (New York: Farrar, Straus and Giroux, 2013).
2. Nagle, *Picking Up,* 16.
3. See Luci Shaw, *Breath for the Bones* (Nashville: Thomas Nelson, 2007), 61.
4. Nagle, *Picking Up,* 25.
5. Plantinga, *Engaging God's World,* 95.
6. Abraham Kuyper, *Calvinism: Six Stone-Lectures,* as quoted in Plantinga, *Engaging God's World,* 95.

CHAPTER 5: THE ICONIC NATURE OF VOCATIONAL PARABLES

1. Gabriel Bunge, *The Rublev Trinity*, translated by Andrew Louth (New York: St. Vladimir's Seminary Press, 2007), 14.
2. My friend and colleague Geoff Vandermolen first brought this vocationally iconic passage to my attention.
3. Bunge, *The Rublev Trinity*, 45.
4. Ibid., 18.
5. Ibid., 18. Italics added.
6. Norman Wirzba, *Food and Faith: A Theology of Eating* (London: Cambridge University Press, 2007), 9–10.
7. Ibid., 10.
8. Ibid., 38.
9. B. Biékowska, ed., C. Cenkalska, trans., *The Scientific World of Copernicus* (Dordrecht, Holland: D. Reidel, 2012), 20.

CHAPTER 6: GOD MADE ALL THINGS (CREATION)

1. This number includes rocks in the earth's crust, and also a lot of metal (mostly nickel and iron) associated with the earth's core. Information provided by geologist Lee Wamsteeker.
2. In 2012 I worked with several geophysicists to research, write, and preach a sermon funded by the John Templeton Foundation: "Geophysics and the Ground of All Being," YouTube video, 35:52, posted by New Hope Hillside Church Calgary, April 30, 2012, https://www.youtube.com/watch?v=q-9rkwLidxA (accessed October 12, 2016).
3. "Anthropomorphism," in *Eerdmans Bible Dictionary*, ed. Allen C. Myers (Grand Rapids, MI: Eerdmans, 1996), 59.
4. Herman Bavinck, *The Philosophy of Revelation* (New York: Longmans, Green, 1908), 27–28. Italics added.
5. Marilynne Robinson, preface to *John Calvin: Steward of God's Covenant*, ed. John F. Thornton and Susan B. Varenne (New York: Vintage, 2006), xv.
6. Mark Noll, *The Scandal of the Evangelical Mind* (Grand Rapids, MI: Eerdmans, 1994), 51.
7. Jan Veenhof, "Revelation and Common Grace," *The Kuyper Center Review*, vol. 2, ed. John Bowlin (Grand Rapids, MI: Eerdmans, 2011), 4.

CHAPTER 7: SIN DISTORTS ALL THINGS (FALL)

1. For more details on the corrupting, perverting, and polluting ways of sin, see Cornelius Plantinga Jr., *Not the Way It's Supposed to Be: A Breviary of Sin* (Grand Rapids, MI: Eerdmans, 1995).
2. C. S. Lewis, *Mere Christianity* (New York: HarperCollins, 2001), 128.
3. Ibid., 121.
4. Andrew Vander Leek, "The Ins and Outs of Doctrinal Preaching" (workshop lectures, Kings University, Edmonton, Alberta, February 16–20, 1987). Vander Leek attributes this quotation to Cornelius Plantinga Jr.
5. Lewis, *Mere Christianity*, 124.
6. Michael Eric Dyson, *Pride: The Seven Deadly Sins* (New York: Oxford University Press, 2006). He wrote this about the sin of racial pride, but his words offer a wonderful corrective to our interactions with anyone, anywhere.
7. Henry Fairlie, *The Seven Deadly Sins Today* (Notre Dame, IN: Notre Dame Press, 1979), 143.

8. Vander Leek, "Ins and Outs of Doctrinal Preaching." Quotation attributed to Cornelius Plantinga Jr.

9. Fredric Jameson, *Postmodernism, or, The Cultural Logic of Late Capitalism* (Durham, NC: Duke University Press, 1991), 206.

10. "Daniel Pink—Autonomy, Mastery & Purpose," YouTube video, 5:11, posted by sonabasu, January 4, 2012, https://www.youtube.com/watch?v=wdzHgN7_Hs8.

11. Peter Corrigan, *The Sociology of Consumption: An Introduction* (London: Sage Publications, 1997), 20, citing the ideas of Jean Baudrillard, *The Consumer Society*, translated by Chris Turner (London: Sage Publications, 1988).

12. Lesslie Newbigin, *Sin and Salvation* (Eugene, OR: Wipf and Stock, 2009), 12.

13. Cornelius Plantinga Jr. commented on how Jesus' atoning sacrifice brings glory to God: "God's splendor becomes clearer whenever God or the Son of God powerfully spends himself in order to cause others to flourish." See Cornelius Plantinga Jr., *Engaging God's World: A Christian Vision of Faith, Learning, and Living* (Grand Rapids, MI: Eerdmans, 2002), 20.

14. Vander Leek, "Ins and Outs of Doctrinal Preaching." Quotation attributed to Cornelius Plantinga Jr.

15. Ibid.

16. Robert McCracken, *What Is Sin? What Is Virtue?* (New York: Harper and Row, 1966), 31.

17. Vander Leek, "Ins and Outs of Doctrinal Preaching." Quotation attributed to Cornelius Plantinga Jr.

18. "List of Federal Political Sex Scandals in the United States," Wikipedia, last modified November 10, 2016, https://en.wikipedia.org/wiki/List_of_federal_political_sex _scandals_in_the_United_States. Italics added.

19. Vander Leek, "Ins and Outs of Doctrinal Preaching." Quotation attributed to Cornelius Plantinga Jr.

20. Plantinga, *Not the Way It's Supposed to Be*, 46.

21. Rob Bell, *Sex God: Exploring the Endless Connections between Sexuality and Spirituality* (Grand Rapids, MI: Zondervan, 2007), 28.

22. *Oxford English Dictionary*, s.v. "Envy," as quoted in Maria Konnikova, "Can Envy Be Good for You?", *The New Yorker*, August 10, 2015, http://www.newyorker.com /science/maria-konnikova/can-envy-be-good-for-you.

23. Joseph Epstein, *Envy: The Seven Deadly Sins* (New York: Oxford University Press, 2003), 19–20.

24. John Calvin wrote, "Even if for a single moment [God] withdrew his supportive hand, the universe would collapse." Quoted by Dale Cooper, "How Carefully God Watches," *Banner*, January 18, 2011, http://www.thebanner.org/departments /2011/01/how-carefully-god-watches.

CHAPTER 8: GOD IS SAVING ALL THINGS (REDEMPTION)

1. Gordon Pitts, "Flying to the Rescue in a Health-Care-Challenged World," *Globe and Mail*, August 1, 2011, http://www.theglobeandmail.com/report-on-business /careers/careers-leadership/flying-to-the-rescue-in-a-health-care-challenged-world /article4259394/. See more about STARS at http://www.stars.ca/ab/.

2. This is a composite of several of the stories told to me by City of Calgary firefighters.

3. Lester DeKoster, *Work: The Meaning of Your Life* (Grand Rapids, MI: Christian's Library Press, 2010), 2, 3–4, 5, 6.

CHAPTER 9: GOD WILL MAKE ALL THINGS NEW (NEW EARTH)

1. John Van Sloten, "Heaven on Earth," *Banner*, August 13, 2012, http://www
.thebanner.org/features/2012/08/heaven-on-earth.
2. Laura Merzig Fabrycky, quoting Tim Keller, in "Ascension and Vocation,"
Washington Institute for Faith, *Vocation and Culture*, May 27, 2014, http://www
.washingtoninst.org/8050/ascension-and-vocation. Italics in original.
3. N. T. Wright, interview by Trevin Wax, "Trevin Wax Interview with N. T.
Wright on *Surprised by Hope*," *The Gospel Coalition*, April 24, 2008, https://blogs
.thegospelcoalition.org/trevinwax/2008/04/24/trevin-wax-interview-with-nt-wright
-on-surprised-by-hope/. Italics added.
4. Plantinga, *Not the Way It's Supposed to Be*, 10.
5. Scot McKnight, "Justice, Righteousness," *Dictionary of Jesus and the Gospels*, eds. Joel
B. Green, Scot McKnight, and I. Howard Marshall (Downers Grove, IL: InterVarsity,
1992), 411.
6. Darrell Cosden, *The Heavenly Good of Earthly Work* (Peabody, MA: Hendrickson,
2006), 2.
7. Miroslav Volf, *Work in the Spirit: Toward a Theology of Work* (Eugene, OR: Wipf and
Stock, 2001), 93.
8. Theologian Jürgen Moltmann first introduced me to the idea of a God who calls us
into the future fulfillment of his Kingdom. God's promises pull us.
9. John Bentley Mays, "One Catholic—in the Darkest Hour," *The Globe
and Mail*, April 2, 2010, http://www.theglobeandmail.com/news/
national/one-catholic---in-the-darkest-hour/article4352621/?page=all.
10. Jim Leech and Jacquie McNish, "The Third Rail: New Brunswick's Electrifying Pension
-Plan Revival," *The Globe and Mail*, May 30, 2014, http://www.theglobeandmail.com
/report-on-business/the-thirdz-rail-new-brunswicks-electrifying-pension-plan-revival
/article18929951/?page=1.
11. Ibid.

CHAPTER 10: STEPPING INTO THE STORY THAT IS YOUR JOB

1. Jason McMartin, "Sleep, Sloth, and Sanctification," *Journal of Spiritual Formation
and Soul Care* 6, no. 2 (Fall 2013): 255–272.
2. The science of epigenetics provides biological proof that the sins of the fathers are,
to some degree, passed on to the children.
3. "Name," in *Eerdmans Bible Dictionary*, ed. Myers, 747.

CHAPTER 11: EMPLOYING THE GIFT OF GRATITUDE

1. John Calvin, quoted in Don Postema, *Space for God: The Study and Practice of
Spirituality* (Grand Rapids, MI: Faith Alive Christian Resources, 1997), 80.
2. Postema, *Space for God*, 70.
3. Brother David Steindl-Rast, "A Deep Bow," *Gratefulness*, http://gratefulness.org
/resource/a-deep-bow/ (accessed November 23, 2016), reprinted from *Main Currents
in Modern Thought* 5, vol. 23 (May–June 1967): 129–132.
4. Abraham Kuyper, *To Be Near unto God* (Grand Rapids, MI: Eerdmans, 1918). See
http://www.ccel.org/ccel/kuyper/near.txt.
5. Ibid.
6. Nicholas P. Wolterstorff, *Educating for Life: Reflections on Christian Teaching and
Learning*, ed. Gloria Goris Stronks and Clarence W. Joldersma (Grand Rapids, MI:
Baker Academic, 2002), 272.

CHAPTER 12: SLOWING DOWN, OPENING YOUR EYES, AND SEEING

1. Norman Wirzba, *Food and Faith: A Theology of Eating* (London: Cambridge University Press, 2007), 63.
2. Ibid., 46.
3. Ibid., 56.

CHAPTER 13: BECOMING A VOCATIONAL MYSTIC

1. Barbara Ehrenreich, *Living with a Wild God: A Nonbeliever's Search for the Truth about Everything* (New York: Hachette, 2014), 115–116.
2. John Calvin, quoted by Marilynne Robinson, preface to *John Calvin: Steward of God's Covenant*, ed. John F. Thornton and Susan B. Varenne (New York: Vintage, 2006), xii–xiii.
3. Kate Taylor, "What Happens When an Atheist Sees God?", *Globe and Mail*, April 4, 2014, http://www.theglobeandmail.com/life/relationships/what-happens -when-an-atheist-sees-god/article17834607/?page=all.
4. Matt Taibbi, "The Great American Bubble Machine," *Rolling Stone*, April 5, 2010, http://www.rollingstone.com/politics/news/the-great-american-bubble-machine -20100405.
5. Lord Brian Griffiths, quoted in "Lord Brian Griffiths: British Economist Offers Perspective on Global Crisis," *Ethix*, February 1, 2010, http://ethix.org/2010/02/01 /lord-brian-griffiths-british-economist-offers-perspective-on-global-crisis.
6. Lesslie Newbigin, *Proper Confidence: Faith, Doubt, and Certainty in Christian Discipleship* (Grand Rapids, MI: Eerdmans, 1995), 10.

CHAPTER 14: TRUSTING THAT GOD WILL USE YOUR WORK

1. Kuyper, *Wisdom and Wonder*, 55.
2. Modris Eksteins, "J'accuse Encore," *Globe and Mail*, October 9, 2009, http://www .theglobeandmail.com/arts/books-and-media/review-why-the-dreyfus-affair-matters -by-louis-begley/article4290570/ (accessed November 23, 2016).
3. Alain de Botton, *The Pleasures and Sorrows of Work* (New York: Vintage, 2009).
4. Susan VanZanten, "Discovering and Uncovering Truth and Beauty," *Comment*, September 14, 2012, https://www.cardus.ca/comment/article/3517/discovering -and-uncovering-truth-and-beauty/.
5. Richard Sennett, *The Craftsman* (New Haven, CT: Yale University Press, 2008), 70.
6. John Donne, *Devotions upon Emergent Occasions and Death's Duel*, ed. Andrew Motion (New York: Vintage, 1999), 100.
7. *Searching for Sugar Man*, directed by Malik Bendjelloul (New York: Sony Pictures Classics, 2012), DVD.
8. Ibid.